Wet and Wild Puppy Grooming

A Complete Training Manual

Jackie Larocque, CPG, CPT

Copyright 2011 Jackie Larocque

All rights reserved. No part of this book may be reproduced, stored in a retrieval system, or transmitted in any form or by any means, electronic, mechanical, recording or otherwise, without the prior written permission of the author.

Published by Red Willow Publishing

ISBN: 978-1-936539-30-7

Dedication

Buffy, Quila, Toshi, Kitt, Boo, Jake and Skye,
thank you for taking me on the greatest leash free walk of my life.

Foreword

When Jackie approached me to have a look at a book she had written on puppy grooming, I knew I was in for treat! I realized this because back some time ago, I was Jackie's grooming instructor, and since that time, I have come to know Jackie as a fountain of knowledge in all things 'doggie'!

In writing this book, Jackie has shared her many years of training and knowledge in a no nonsense, progressive manner, while keeping the contents an enjoyable read. The learning part quietly settled in while I was simply enjoying her book.

Jackie has written with some focus on the professional groomer, however anyone with an interest or love of puppies and their care, will greatly benefit from all chapters. Whether focused on the raising, breeding, behaviour, or grooming aspect, we can all learn something valuable about puppies from Jackie.

I would recommend this book to the professional, novice and puppy owner alike. I know that the knowledge imparted from the earliest stages of a puppy's life onwards will be beneficial to each, in one way or another. Not only will you gain some serious puppy knowledge from Jackie's book, you'll enjoy the journey, as well

I'll be recommending this book to my future grooming students.

Nice job, Jackie!

Joy Waters, CPGI, DCPG
Author of JKL's Homestudy of Professional Grooming
Owner/Instructor of JKL Pet Groomer Training Academy
www.jklgrooming.com

Acknowledgements

First and foremost, I acknowledge all the puppies (now dogs) that were part of the development of this book. They taught me the most about different personalities, traits, and how to handle them. I wish I could name them all, but it would fill several pages.

A special thank you to my husband and kids, Stephan, Tachara, Sulley, and Kiara, for putting up with my constant badgering in helping with the photos as well as putting up with me ignoring them while I worked on this book.

A big furry thank you to groomers, Kelli Norris, Laryssa Pugh, Valerie Ferguson, Jacqueline Parsons, and Joy Waters for reading this book and giving me valuable input.

Chris O'Byrne, thank you for editing this book and your patience for guiding me down the publishing road, I know I was a P.I.T.A.

And last but not least, Ralphie. Who acted like a puppy through the hundred or so snapshots for the cover of this book.

Table of Contents

INTRODUCTION 1

CHAPTER 1 Where Do Puppies Come From 3
Pet stores 3
Puppy mills 3
Puppy farms 4
Hobby breeders 5
Professional breeders 5
Home breeders 6
Humane Society/SPCA 6

CHAPTER 2 Puppy Stages 7
Conception 7
Pregnancy 8
Birth to three weeks 8
Three to seven weeks 8
Eight to twelve weeks 9
Fear imprint eight to eleven weeks 9
Twelve to fifteen weeks 10
Sixteen to twenty weeks 10
Twenty to twenty four weeks 10

CHAPTER 3 Temperaments and Personalities 11
Temperaments 12
Personalities 14

CHAPTER 4 Techniques 17
Operant Conditioning 17
Positive Reinforcement 17
Shake a Paw 17
Negative Reinforcement 18
Positive Punishment 18
Negative Punishment 18
Classical Conditioning 18
Shaping 18
Luring 20
In the shop 20

Chapter 5 First Puppy Groom 23

Rewards, discipline and bribes 23
Meet and greet the puppy 24
Let's groom 25
Ready for puppy? 26
Pre-bath 39
Troubleshooting table work 43
The bath 45
Troubleshooting the bath 49
Finishing 50
Troubleshooting the finish 58
Homework for owners 62

Chapter 6 Second Visit 65

Meet and greet 65
Hydraulic table 66
Steps/ramp 69
Pre-bath groom 69
Touch and feel 70
Positions 70
Nail grinder 72
Clippers 73
What to expect 74
Troubleshooting 75
Bath 79
Troubleshooting the bath 80
High voltage dryer 81
Finishing 81
Troubleshooting the finish 83
Homework For owners 85

Chapter 7 The Third Visit 87

Troubleshooting 92

Chapter 8 Quick Glance Reference 95

First visit 95
Second visit 95
Third visit 95

Chapter 9 Setting up The Program 97

Chapter 10 Marketing the Program 99

Chapter 11 Toes and Tails 103

About the Author 105

Photo Credits 106

Resources 112

Introduction

Grooming a puppy is like painting a picture during an earthquake. Not only does it take patience and skill, having a sense of humour doesn't hurt, either. Young puppies are learning vast amounts of information while developing, and the first or second experience in a grooming shop can dictate how the puppy will react in grooming shops for the remainder of his life. The grooming community has not addressed the most important process of grooming: the process of teaching a puppy the grooming process in a consistent, positive, step by step program. The teaching of puppies in a grooming shop was left solely up to the groomers; however not every groomer is a dog trainer. Some groomers have a knack with puppies; others do not.

The most difficult thing to remember is the four month old Great Dane, who can barely fit into your tub, is still a puppy. As groomers, we are in a very precarious position with puppies that can affect how the puppy reacts to the grooming process throughout its life as an adult dog.

When I started grooming dogs I had already been a professional dog trainer for 15 years. I was comfortable working with behaviour dogs and developed different techniques based on individual dogs to modify certain behaviours. Working at vet clinics also expanded my knowledge of animals and taught me different perspectives on how dogs and cats behave in stressful situations. Combining my knowledge and experiences, and bringing it into the grooming shop for the last 14 years has aided me in avoiding many bite wounds, (having quick reflexes didn't hurt either).

I found a common thread with many of the behaviour dogs with respect to grooming. The majority of them had one or more bad experiences in a grooming shop as puppies. I searched for a course on grooming puppies and to my great disappointment; there wasn't a step by step program strictly for puppies. I experimented and develop this program over five years. I have been tweaking and modifying a puppy program to teach to other groomers. My aim was to develop a program to prevent puppies and groomers from having bad experiences in the grooming shops that would follow not only the dogs, but also the owners and each groomer that tried to groom them afterwards.

This program is designed to enable all groomers or pet owners to train a puppy to be groomed. Many of the components of this program can be integrated into puppy training classes to further aid in the grooming process. Some of the methods in the puppy program can be transferred to adult dogs for rehabilitation in the grooming shop as well.

Different components are taught during each visit with a repetition of the previous visits. Equipment, positioning, and commands are taught in a safe step by step method to the puppy. This minimizes injury to the puppy as well as stress. Grooming doesn't have to be a fearful, stressful event in a dogs' life and if taught in a relaxed gradual manner, puppies that experience the puppy program become the easiest dogs to groom before they reach adulthood.

The puppies are trained over two to three visits; each visit occurs four to five weeks apart. The earliest I start a puppy in the program is twelve weeks and the latest I will accept them into the program is five months. Age and breed will determine whether I put them through a two or three visit program. A puppy at five months is more emotionally and mentally mature than a puppy of three months and can handle larger chunks of learning and I will combine visit one and two into a single visit. A German Shepherd puppy will have less grooming requirements than a Poodle; therefore, I will offer a two-visit puppy program for the low maintenance breeds and a three-visit program for the high maintenance breeds.

After learning the puppy program, you will be able to explain to potential customers exactly what their puppy is going to learn in each visit. This will put the customers at ease, as I find there is a lot of grey area with a bath and tidy. Different shops will give different answers to potential customers as to exactly what the puppy is taught if anything. With the puppy program, 95% of the puppies will stand still and let you groom them by the time they are six months old. This saves you time and energy and builds your client base as most customers with puppies will stay with you after the puppy program.

The program takes into consideration the stage of emotional development, temperament, personality and breed. Each chapter has a troubleshooting guide for different problems you may encounter and also includes homework for owners. There is a quick glance chapter at the end that outlines each visit in point form.

I will go over different problems the puppies may present and how to trouble shoot those problems. We will cover why it is important to run a puppy program and why it is successful, both for the puppy and for your business.

There is also a chapter on setting up the program for your shop and how to market your puppy program for added income.

I'm not going to tell you the different styles to use on different breeds, but I am going to teach you how to train a puppy to be groomed correctly.

Honestly, I would be happy if my business had a plummet in behaviour dogs that came to my shop.

Are you ready to delve into the world of puppies?

Chapter 1 Where Do Puppies Come From

Okay, aside from the obvious place where all puppies come from, where else do puppies come from? Genetics as well as environment can dictate how a puppy will react and behave in stressful situations. No matter how calm your shop is, the puppy will still be under stress. Let's investigate different environments and how it can affect the puppy sniffing around your shop.

Pet stores

Let's be honest here—most puppies in large chain pet stores come from either puppy mills or puppy farms. The pet stores do not buy directly from the puppy mills, but through a puppy broker. But the end result is they come from the mills.

Pet stores excel at socializing these puppies. They get handled by many customers of all ages and ethnic backgrounds and also by the staff. I have yet to see any staff member in a pet store be cruel to a puppy. They love them and handle them with care and attention. Most of the puppies have had their first bath and some may have been partially shaved.

Puppy mills

We see the pictures and watch the videos on the news and it gives us an idea of what is commonly referred to as puppy mills. Pictures and videos do not do it justice. If you want to fully experience a puppy mill, contact your local SPCA or Humane Society to give you a call to volunteer should they ever shut one down.

Hundreds of dogs tucked into small cages stacked on top of one another. There can be anywhere from three to six dogs in a cage. Of course the dogs on the bottom get much of the waste, feces and urine from the dogs above them as it falls through the grates on the bottom of the cage. Each cage will usually contain three to five females and one to two males, as well as puppies that are in the process of being born or are already born.

Puppy mills are just that, they mill puppies. There is very little consideration in the breeding and care of the brood bitches or studs. They have uncontrolled breeding and often puppies are classed as Shih Tzu type or Terrier type.

From the first moment of conception, puppy mill puppies have the potential to be behaviour challenged. They take more time and patience to train. This is generally speaking. I have met some puppy mill puppies that are wonderful, but I've met many more who are not.

Puppy mill puppies have had very little socialization while in the mill and have had very little or no grooming experience until they arrive at the pet store. The first brief encounter with humans has been at feeding time and often the first physical interaction with humans is when the puppy mill owner grabs them from their mother to ship them to a broker. Puppy mills produce puppies on a large scale; many of the puppies have genetic diseases or behavioural problems. It is estimated that over half a million puppies come from puppy mills per year in the United States.

The driving force is money.

Many areas have very few requirements for pet owners. As long as the dog has food, water and shelter, the requirements have been met. SPCA and Humane society workers get very frustrated, as they are unable to shut down large operations of puppy mills because of the skeletal requirements for dog breeding facilities in many areas.

Puppy farms

What is the difference between a puppy farm and a puppy mill? Not much. Puppy farms generally will be on a smaller scale with 20 to 70 dogs. Dogs are kept in large pens or stalls, generally split into two-three groups and have uncontrolled breeding, where several males can breed one female and the bitch is bred every heat cycle. Puppy farms will usually sell directly to the pet store rather than go through a broker or will advertise in the paper and sell directly to the public. Puppy farms will advertise themselves as breeders. They will generally focus on one or two breeds or the cross of those breeds. Many farms will offer a handy service of picking out the puppy for you and bringing it to you so you don't have to be inconvenience by travelling out to them. This service guarantees that the prospective customer can't see the condition of the puppy farm or the dogs. When prospective customers phone a puppy farm, the customers will ask if they have any Pomeranian-Poodle crosses. The farms will tell the customer that they do. The customer then calls you with their new pom/poo cross. They come for their appointment and in walks a Terrier cross.

Puppies from farms have had little socialization with people. Some may have been handled briefly; some may not. The shy puppies tend to hide and therefore will not have been handled. Most have not experienced any of the grooming process or have had a quick bath. Again, the driving force for puppy farms is money.

Hobby breeders

Nowadays, however, we have to be careful when we hear "from a breeder". There is a new term: Hobby Breeder. They used to be called backyard breeders, but have changed the name to be more aesthetically appealing. The word breeder gives customers a sense of security and confidence that if they are a breeder, they are knowledgeable. Hobby breeders will range from 6 to 20 dogs.

They usually focus on mixed breeds and are usually small dogs. They advertise with designer names; Chorkies (Chihuahua-Yorkie cross) PomaPoo (Pomeranian-Poodle cross) Bichon-Shih Tzu cross, Labradoodle (Labrador Retriever-Poodle cross), Terripoo (Terrier-Poodle cross) Shug (Pug Shih Tzu cross), Puddle (Pug Poodle cross) these are only a few and I have to admit, it is fun coming up with names for some of the mixes that come in. Hobby breeders will often have one to four males to service the bitches. The puppies generally get better husbandry than the mills or farms and are often kept in the house. However, the main driving force is money. They often have uncontrolled breeding or they breed without any consideration for genetic traits that will be passed on. They too advertise themselves as breeders and will sell a Terrier cross to a customer that wants a Pom-Poo. They will tell customers that are looking for a non-shedding Labradoodle that their puppies don't shed, when in fact the owner winds up with a Labradoodle that sheds more than a regular lab.

Depending on the size of the hobby breeder, puppies from hobby breeders may have experienced a bath and been handled. If they are raised in the house, they have experienced sounds and sights of a household environment. There are hobby breeders that are conscientious breeders, but not many. Again, the driving force is money.

Professional breeders

Professional breeders choose the bitch and stud through researching genetics and temperament to improve their line, eliminating medical or behaviour traits, while at the same time illuminating the strengths. They usually have two to ten dogs on their premises and enter their dogs and puppies at dog shows on a regular basis. A professional breeder is someone who can tell you exactly what physical problems are in the line and which generation the physical issue appeared. The dogs are registered, or the owner has the option of having the puppy registered with the governing kennel club of the country the puppy was born in. Breeders care very much where the puppies are going and in many cases prospective owners are required to fill out paperwork, sign contracts, and make a few trips to the breeder before they take the puppy. The driving force is to breed a stable dog for competition.

Puppies from professional breeders are by far the easiest puppies to teach the grooming process to. They are used to being handled, have already been introduced to a grooming table, brushes, combs, a bath, dryer and the sound of the clippers. They have had a wide variety of experiences of the world around them and are raised in a healthy, stable environment.

Home breeders

Home breeders usually own one to five dogs. They breed on a very small scale and will usually breed either one unregistered breed or a particular mixed breed, Bichon-Shih Tzu crosses for example. The breeding dogs are pets and are cared for as such. They usually have the parents and one or two puppies from previous litters that they've kept. They may be choosy as to whom the puppies go to. They will advertise on flyers in the district where they live or put an ad in the local paper. For home breeders, the driving force is the demand: people that want a puppy from their dog. They tend to put a lot of thought into having another litter as they have experienced how much work it is. This can be translated into they put a lot of work into each litter. Puppies from home breeders tend to be well-adjusted puppies that are easy to groom from day one. Many of them have experienced a bath and possibly a dryer and a brush. They are used to being handled by a variety of people.

Humane Society/SPCA

Puppies from the Humane Societies or SPCAs are usually surrendered, rescued, or from a pregnant bitch has found her way to the center. Many societies now have foster homes for young puppies to be raised until they are eligible for adoption. They may or may not have experienced grooming equipment. I treat these puppies the same as a home breeder puppy.

Please note there are exceptions to the descriptions above. These explanations are general, not specific.

Why is it important to puppy grooming to know where the puppy came from? Where the puppy comes from can dictate how we handle the puppy. If a puppy is from a puppy mill, we can assume that this puppy will have confidence issues and possibly physical issues and may be more cautious or scared. A scared puppy may bite. On the other hand, a puppy from a professional breeder will be less shy about the equipment and handling. Puppies from puppy mills, farms, and hobby breeders will require more patience and you will have to go at a slower pace than puppies from home breeders or professional breeders.

Chapter 2 Puppy Stages

As puppies mature through different stages, they exhibit different behaviours. Knowing what stage the puppy on your table is in aids how you will handle the puppy and also what you can expect.

Conception

Let's start at the very beginning—conception.

Typically, a bitch will be in heat for 21 days. The first stage is proestrus. This is where they bleed, the vulva swells, and they secrete pheromones to attract males. But they won't accept a male. Typically this can last between four to nine days.

The second stage is estruses or standing heat. The bleeding usually stops, the secretions change, and the bitch will accept a male. Typically this stage lasts 4 to 13 days.

The last two stages are metestrus and anestrous. This is the wind down of the heat cycle, and although there is ovarian activity, the vulva gradually returns to normal size and secretions stop.

The stage we are concerned with is the second stage: estruses. This is when new puppies are made; the moment of conception.

This stage will determine the development or lack of development of puppies in utero.

Scenario:

The bitch goes into standing heat on day 7 of her heat cycle and is bred on that day and on day 8. She is not bred again until day 11. Each day she is bred, she conceives two puppies.

Puppies conceived on day 7 have a 4-day head start on development over puppies conceived on day 11. However, labour is dictated by the puppies that are conceived first. This is how runts are made. They are smaller and weaker and will develop mentally and physically a few days later than the first puppies. This does not mean that runts are sickly, just that they are behind in development.

Pregnancy

While the puppies are developing, they are learning about the world outside through their mother. Is the bitch in a healthy environment? Does the bitch live in fear? Is she fed healthy food? All of this information transfers to the puppies about the world they are about to be born into. I have found that puppies that come from a healthy environment both physically and emotionally are easier to groom. Puppies that are born to bitches that are groomed on a regular basis, including when they are pregnant, are easier to groom. They have already experienced the vibration and feel of the clippers, bath, and dryer through their mom.

Puppies that come from puppy mills, puppy farms, or hobby breeders are more difficult. They have lived three months feeling everything their mother has including, poor maintenance, fear and no socialization.

This poses a very important question to the new puppy owner standing in your shop, "Where did you get the puppy?"

Birth to three weeks

The puppy's ears and eyes are closed. They are learning about the world around them through smell, feel, and taste. Their eyes and ears will open between the second and third week. As their eyesight and hearing develops, so does their mobility. Their main focus is to eat, gain weight, and sleep.

Three to seven weeks

A whole new world is opening up as their vision clears by five weeks. Curiosity comes into play and puppies investigate their surroundings. Littermates and mother become play things, as do any humans available. This is an important stage of socialization. They learn the rules of play, inhibited biting (not to bite too hard), to walk, run, wag their tail, bark, and puppy games. Between five to seven weeks they learn doggie manners from their mom. This is the stage where she will become a little gruffer with them. Puppies start to learn what is acceptable and what is not. They learn respect. At seven weeks, puppy's temperaments have come into full bloom.

Eight to twelve weeks

Puppies are gaining more control over their physical capabilities, coordination is improving and ranks among the puppies have been established. Puppies are learning incredible amounts in this stage. I like to call this the sponge stage. They are soaking up information and keeping it. What they learn during this stage stays with them for their life. This is the best time to start socializing a puppy with new environments, people and experiences.

Fear imprint eight to eleven weeks

This is one of the most important stages in the puppy's development. Eight weeks is the standard age for fear imprint. Fear imprint may start during the eighth week period and carry on into the tenth week period. Remember, time of conception can determine development timing. Breed can also determine emotional development. Smaller breeds tend to develop physically and emotionally sooner than large or giant breeds. If a puppy gets very frightened at this stage, for example at a sudden loud noise, the fear makes an imprint on them and they will be fearful of loud noises for the rest of their lives. It's very important not to overwhelm a puppy during this time, as a series of events can turn a puppy that would normally be happy and outgoing into a timid, fearful puppy.

Twelve to fifteen weeks

This stage is where the puppy's personality starts to become clear. They start to test their owners and their environment. They learn to use their growl and biting in appropriate situations. For instance, a play growl is different than an angry growl. A puppy at twelve weeks is still unsure of new situations, but will have the courage to investigate. The first puppy groom should start here. They accept you will not hurt them and are fairly easy to deal with.

Sixteen to twenty weeks

A puppy at 16 weeks is much more confident than a twelve week old puppy and will investigate with confidence. They challenge with more intention and have no problem snapping or fighting if you are doing something they don't like. They are in the beginning stages of puberty. Sexual awareness starts. Males start to mark and humping becomes an annoying habit. They realize that they have choices and can control the out come. This is the time where they start rebelling, running away from their owners, playing the "catch me if you can game". They learn both good and bad consequences of their actions. Biting becomes more serious and intentional.

The second groom should take place at or after 16 weeks. If a groomer handles this age aggressively or roughly, it will cause problems in subsequent grooms. This age is the hardest to groom. The puppy will fight you as he struggles with the choice of allowing you to groom him or not. This stage requires patience, praise, and a bit more discipline.

Twenty to twenty four weeks
Puppies have become more secure in their environment. They are independent in their thinking and make calculated decisions. They understand trust and the breaking of trust. In the last stages of adolescence, the males are marking purposefully. They are learning limits, but still testing their family and people around them to see what they can get away with. They invent different ways to avoid things and become sneaky about testing limits. For example, if they don't like their butt being touched, they will sit rather than bite. They have learned bite inhibition, (to bite or not or how hard to bite). The hormones are settling down and many of the females are approaching their first heat. Their learning mechanism becomes one of understanding, rather than just following the food. There is less rebelling when learning something new as learning becomes fun and builds confidence. The third groom should occur between 20 to 24 four weeks.

Chapter 3 Temperaments and Personalities

Temperaments dictate how the puppy or dog will react in different situations and to different stimuli. Temperament is why your dog is doing what he's doing. At seven weeks, a temperament test can be given to a litter of puppies by a professional dog trainer, (that understands how to do the test and read the results) to determine the temperament traits of that puppy. Many professional breeders will hire a trainer to test a litter to better match a puppy with a person or family.

A temperament test can show if the puppy is forgiving, a trait sought after by obedience trainers, the degree of dominance or submissiveness, if oral (oral dogs will chew, bark and bite), the tenacity of the puppy, whether he recovers from a surprise, and how the puppy will react when presented with new scenarios.

Temperament tests outline the basic traits of the puppy and how he will react to the world around him.

Personality is who your dog is. His quirks, both lovable and annoying, his likes and dislikes. Personalities are forever growing and changing as the puppy grows into adulthood and then senior years. I've outlined some of the more common personalities. Many personalities may overlap or may be combined in a dog. It is common to have a laid-back surfer dog that also has a royalty complex.

Temperaments

Dependant vs. independent

Dependant puppies follow humans readily. They are usually eager to please and willing learners. However, extremely dependant puppies may become nervous when separated from humans, and can become barkers or whiners in kennels. Independent puppies come to you when they are ready and are more hesitant to follow. They have a higher degree of dominance than dependant puppies and may take more patience to teach. A dependant puppy will trust you and accept new positions and equipment easily where as an independent puppy will be suspicious.

Forgiving vs. non-forgiving

A forgiving puppy will forgive you readily should you hurt him. He always gives you second and third chances and rarely holds a grudge. A non-forgiving puppy will need some time before he will forgive you. If you hurt this puppy, for example if you pull on a mat too hard, he may growl if you try to release the matt again, he may move his body so it is difficult for you to access the mat, and he may even snap at you. If a puppy is showing these behaviours after you may have pulled the fur too hard or clipped a nail too short, move to a different area of the body to work on or put the puppy off the table to allow him time to forgive you. It is rare that you find a puppy that is completely non-forgiving. Non-forgiving puppies hold grudges and if you force him, without allowing the puppy time to forgive, you will create problems.

Elevation

Puppies that exhibit strong leadership qualities (dominance), will react strongly on the table by tensing, struggling, fighting etc. If you use a noose, they will fight the noose and scream and claw at it. You have to be calm and assertive with these puppies. The table is the place above all other places in the grooming shop that these puppies must respect you and respect your rules and leadership. It is not necessary that you pin these puppies; in fact, I strongly suggest you don't. Growling or any deep guttural noise is sufficient to get your point across. They will not readily accept you training them on the table, but be consistent and repetitive. They will eventually accept what you are teaching them, they just have to argue with you for a bit. You may find that you get better result by doing much of the grooming (nails, ear plucking) with this type of puppy in your lap for the first two visits. Always praise the puppy when he is accepting what you are showing or doing to him, even if the acceptance is very minute.

Touch sensitivity
Puppies that exhibit strong touch sensitivity will need more repetition of everything in the puppy program. Their skin almost crawls when you touch them and they wiggle and spin with every hair brushed or clipped. Touch sensitive puppies behave as if everything tickles and in a sense he does. They will react as if the water coming from the sprayer is stabbing them. It is much the same as if you have a sunburn and your skin is sensitive to everything.

Sound sensitivity
Puppies with strong sound sensitivity will shake, urinate, scream, spin, or jump at sudden or loud sounds. All equipment should be introduced with the sound away from this puppy, gradually moving the sound closer to him. Sound sensitive puppies should be given time to adjust to the sound and be allowed to investigate the object with the sound off and on. High velocity dryers should not be used on sound sensitive puppies during the puppy program. However, the puppy should be exposed to the sound throughout the program.

For extremely sound sensitive puppies, plugging the ears with cotton balls can minimize the stress created by the equipment in the shop.

Sight sensitivity
Puppies that have strong sight sensitivity will be very interested in moving objects. They will have different degrees of reactions—from investigating with curiosity to biting at the object to complete fear of the object. Sight sensitive puppies that exhibit fear will freeze, duck or urinate at moving objects in the grooming shop such as scissors, clippers or water from the hose. Puppies that are on the other end of the scale will attack the brush, clippers, or water and may even try to eat the dryer. When introducing a new piece of equipment, let these puppies see the equipment, let them sniff, lick and give a bit of a chew before you start moving him. Once he is moving, let him sniff, lick, or chew the object again. Expect sight sensitive puppies to attack the spray from the hose and the air from the dryer.

There are other components to a temperament test, but these are the main temperament components that we are concerned with in the grooming shop.

Personalities

Tough guy

This is the puppy that walks in and owns the place. He is friendly, but will also try to push you around. He will growl or bite you if you are doing something he doesn't like. Don't mistake growling or biting for aggression—it's not with this type of puppy. He wants things his way and tends to be bossy. He will growl, but much of the growling is more talking than warning. Until you have a solid relationship with this type of puppy, watch for snapping. This puppy will push the limits and will fight if approached aggressively with training. The nice thing about this personality is that once the boundaries are set, they respect them. They are smart, they are tough, and if you say *No* they won't collapse in a heap on the table and urinate. They use growling and biting to back you off. You must be consistent with this personality. Praise is the key with tough guys. If you meet his growling with aggression, he will bite. Be stern, but positive.

Wild ones

These puppies are wild. Staying still for even two seconds is hard for them. Everything is more with the wild ones. They tend to be overdramatic, ultra sensitive, and would rather jump, run, and play than anything else. Their focus changes very quickly. Wild ones will investigate everything with enthusiasm and all of their senses. They will taste, chew, pounce, throw, listen, and roll on an object before they are satisfied that they have investigated it completely. They're into everything and are so enthusiastic about life that they are charming, but they can be a happy handful. Wild ones have a very good sense of humour, but they can also be easily crushed emotionally. When mistreated, they will show it with their whole body. They will crawl, urinate, roll over, and tuck their tail under. A dog with this personality that has been mistreated in a grooming shop will display these behaviours upon entering the shop. It is best to be very calm with this personality, keep your voice quiet and talk minimally. Wild ones may be wild in the shop until they reach seven to eight months.

Laid back surfer dude

We all love these mellow, always happy puppies. You can do anything and they take it all in stride. They don't hold grudges, but will become wary if they are hurt. They will do anything asked of them as long as it doesn't put them in danger. It takes a lot to get a puppy with this personality to react negatively. If they feel unsafe, they will show it in their body language by crouching, licking, and crawling. Stay very relaxed with the surfer dudes. If you are overly jubilant, they will be suspicious.

Royalty (prince or princess)

These puppies have an air of royalty about them. They like to look good. Royalty puppies will not bite unless you aren't heeding their warnings. They expect to be treated with respect. They are very definite as to what and whom they like. They hold individual grudges. For example, if they had a groomer they didn't like, they won't hold it against you. They can be a bit stand-offish until they are sure they can trust you.

Act in a professional, businesslike way. This personality is a no-nonsense type of dog.

Love puppy

Love puppies are very forgiving. If you pull a bit too hard on a mat, they will swing around, jump on you, and lick you to death to show they forgive you. These puppies may be nervous high-energy dogs and if unsure how to react, they always fall back on licking. Very rarely will these puppies bite or even growl. The biggest reward for them is to be allowed to lick you without limitations. Act business-like and use praise only when you are ready to be licked.

Cautious puppy

Cautious puppies are unsure. They are wary of new situations and need time to adjust. Definitely a look before they leap type. Once they are confident that the situation is safe, they relax. Everything is followed by a pause with this personality. You must groom them with a calm confidence, but allow them to adjust when you make a change of equipment or position. If a sudden change is made or if you pick them up too suddenly, they will bite without warning. This personality is less stressed if the same routine is followed every groom and they know what to expect.

Scared puppy

Scared puppies will hide or freeze, will usually urinate when picked up, and will probably urinate if you look at them. They will collapse on the table, shake, and probably urinate. It takes a lot for them to move or to be interested in things around them. Fear drives their actions and they will bit if scared enough, but typically they focus on trying to disappear.

Scared puppies need time to adjust to new situations. You must take it slow with this personality and allow them to adjust to every new scenario. A set routine allows this personality to be at ease. Don't talk to them. If you do, keep your voice very quiet.

Mean puppy
These puppies are just plain mean. They will bite indiscriminately. They are food aggressive, toy aggressive, territorial, and will bite anyone at any time with or without warning. These puppies grow up to be dangerous dogs. They are wired that way. Fortunately, truly mean puppies are rare and it is very unlikely you'll ever meet one.

Chapter 4 Techniques

There are many techniques of training or shaping dog behaviour. I won't go into detail on each of these techniques, but I'll give you an overview as to how they work and the meanings of them.

Operant Conditioning

Operant conditioning is consequences. The dog learns there are both positive and negative consequences to his actions either through reinforcers or punishers.

Positive Reinforcement

You are rewarding positive behaviour and ignoring negative behaviour. Positive reinforcement can include praise, both physical and verbal, food, a toy, or play. Positive reinforcement is often used when you have to physically manipulate the dog into the position you need him to be in. The best way to illustrate this is by an example.

Shake a Paw

To teach a dog to shake a paw:

Have the dog sitting in front or you.

Physically pick up the paw while saying the command, "Shake a paw."

Give the dog a small piece of food and a verbal praise of good dog.

Replace the foot on the floor.

Repeat steps 1–4.

By the third or fourth repetition, the dog will start to move his paw at the command, "Shake a paw."

As soon as the dog moves his paw, reward him.

Gradually expect more from the dog before you give him the reward until he places his paw in your hand for the reward.

If the dog doesn't place his paw in your hand, do not reward him.

The dog learns to work harder for the reward.

Positive reinforcement also works in shaping the behaviour in small increments. The reward can be a variety of articles as not every dog is food orientated.

Negative Reinforcement

Negative reinforcement is where something bad stops or is taken away when the desired behaviour is attained.

If the dog has a pinch or choke collar on and is pulling, the collar tightens uncomfortably around his throat. When he walks beside you, there is no tightening. By walking beside you, the discomfort has been taken away.

Positive Punishment

How can punishment be positive? When we refer to positive punishment, it means the same as stopping unwanted behaviour. The punishment isn't positive, but the result is.

For example, with barking collars a positive punishment is the dog gets a citronella spray when he barks. The punishment is the spray and the positive is he stops unwanted barking.

Negative Punishment

Negative punishment isn't a slap or even a vocal, "No"; it is removing something good.

The puppy is playing too rough, the playing stops. It's that simple.

Classical Conditioning

Classical conditioning is conditioning a certain response with a stimuli. Pavlov demonstrated classical conditioning in his experiment with dogs. He rang a bell whenever he gave them food. The dogs learned that the bell meant food and consequently demonstrated physical reactions to the bell: salivating, excitement, etc.

In a grooming shop, classical conditioning is very apparent.

A dog that has been mistreated in previous grooming shops will exhibit certain behaviours and body language upon entering any grooming shop. The grooming shop becomes the stimuli to set up physical and physiological responses to previous negative experiences.

Classical conditioning can cause either positive or negative reactions to a stimulus.

Shaping

Shaping a desired behaviour (trick, obedience command etc.) is based on a reward for the behaviour. Shaping can also be a form of classical conditioning. Shaping is done in small, gradual steps, building the behaviour up to the desired result. Food is often used as a positive reward and motivator, accompanied by praise, whistle, or a click from a clicker. In essence, the click or whistle, acts as a bridge, telling the dog that his actions are correct, and the reward (food), will come later. Eventually the bridge becomes more important than the actual food reward.

Timing is of utmost importance, which is why a clicker or whistle is used as the noise can be timed almost simultaneously with the behaviour. The sound is more precise in timing than a voice or a piece of food.

Shaping works on the positive behaviour of the dog and increases the willingness for the dog to learn new things as the dog is being rewarded or told, by the click, that he is doing it right, without any lag time between performance and reward.

Shaping also gets the dog thinking and often, dogs will go through a variety of motions or tricks to figure out exactly what you want from him.

If you are interested in implementing clicker training in your shop, it is my suggestion to obtain a foot clicker as it is very difficult to hold a dog, equipment and clicker in your hands at the same time and get your timing right. Another alternative to an actual clicker is to cluck your tongue imitating the sound of an actual clicker.

Clicker training in a grooming shop is also an excellent way to introduce owners into this training method and is very successful if used in the home as well as the grooming shop.

The down side of using this training method in the grooming shop is time. Many groomers just don't have the time required for shaping each behaviour needed in the grooming shop. However, it's an option to present to owners that are interested in clicker training. If you want to offer this option, then it is my suggestion to split up the three-visit puppy program presented in this book into smaller increments. Each visit can be split up into three to five visits over a two-week period with different behaviours shaped and reinforced during the visits. This removes the stress of time management of trying to shape the training in one visit. However, you will have to adjust your pricing accordingly. Clicker training in a grooming shop can be very successful. If you have never had clicker training a dog outside of a grooming shop, it is my suggestion to either take a class on clicker training or to educate yourself with the book, *Don't Shoot The Dog* by Karen Pryor.

Luring
This technique consists of luring the puppy into the position you want him to be. Food is the easiest lure for puppies.

Hold a piece of food in front of the nose and move the food slowly straight up. The puppy's nose will follow it up and the butt will go down into a sit. Lure the food down and away from the puppy—his nose will follow the food and he will move his body into a down position.

Lures can be anything that the puppy wants: food, toy, hand, etc.

Racing dogs, such as greyhounds, chase a mechanical rabbit lure around a track.

In the shop
Throughout this manual, there are examples of all techniques to help you decide which techniques to use.

I don't limit myself to one technique. All puppies are individuals requiring their own technique or techniques. It is important to have a working understanding of training techniques. Where one technique may fail, another one may succeed.

For example:

Barking in the cage. If I ignore the unwanted behaviour of barking, I find that not only does it escalate, but it also increases the stress of each dog in the shop. If I use a positive reinforcer of praise or food when the dog is quiet, I find that in many cases the dog barks and then is quiet to get the food. So I am continually going to the cage to reward it for being quiet, even though the dog is still barking between quiet spells. He has learned that if he barks and then is quiet, he gets the reward. However, if I use a positive punishment of squirting the dog in the face with water whenever the dog barks, he learns that barking gets him squirted, but being quiet removes the water squirting. I use the water squirting in the shop to stop unwanted barking behaviour because it works on a consistent basis.

I use luring to lure puppies into different positions I need them to be in for grooming.

I shape certain behaviours with a reward, such as getting up on the table or into the tub.

Positive reinforcement is used all the time when the dog performs a position or behaviour I am teaching him or asking of him.

Negative punishment is pretty easy on puppies—I simply ignore the puppy. In other words, I take the attention away.

It is not necessary to know all the technical terminology of techniques used in training a dog; however, it is wise to at least become familiar with different techniques and methods to improve communication with the owners and have a more positive working relationship with the dogs.

Chapter 5 First Puppy Groom

The first puppy groom should take place no sooner than 12 weeks. At 12 weeks, the puppy has safely passed through the fear imprint stage. He has probably been removed from the litter and has had time to adjust to his new home. Their immune system is mature and the puppy should have at least one set of vaccination boosters.

Puppies between 12 and 15 weeks are fairly easy to deal with and any problems can be corrected either by you or with help from the owners at home.

The main goal of the first puppy groom is to make the puppy feel safe. Play is an important part of the puppy program. I put all breeds through the puppy program, introducing them to all the noisy tools and the specific tools they will encounter for regular grooming. For short haired and double-coated dogs, introduce the different brushes and deshedding tools they will come in contact with throughout their life.

Rewards, discipline and bribes

Puppies have a very short attention span at this age. Training sessions are short, no longer than ten minutes at a time. Praise the puppy when he has performed the command you have given it. Even if you have to physically manipulate him into a particular position, praise him. Keep rewards mostly praise and save the food for bribing.

Disciplining a puppy is very easy—simply growl. A young puppy doesn't understand what *No* means, but will understand a growl. If you feel embarrassed by growling, a simple *Ack* in a low guttural voice will act the same as a growl. As the puppy grows up, during the second and third visit, scruffing him if he is getting out of control accompanied with a growl or the word *No* growled at him will easily get the message across. Scruffing doesn't mean grabbing him by the scruff and shaking. All you have to do pull up on the scruff a bit and hold the scruff for a few seconds. Screaming at or hitting a puppy is unacceptable.

Do we really need to discipline a puppy? Sometimes we do, but honestly, a simple growl is more than enough to get your point across. The reason that we sometimes have to discipline is simply a matter of safety. If you are training for obedience, it is often more advantageous to ignore the unwanted behaviour and concentrate on the wanted behaviour. However in a grooming shop, if a puppy starts to flail his head around as you are trimming the hair around his eyes, the risk for injury heightens. He must learn that unwanted behaviour will eventually be disciplined. It's a matter of safety. Puppies understand a growl and a glare. They don't understand getting screamed at, shaken, or hit, but they will learn that grooming is a bad thing, something to be feared. A growl or a growl accompanied with a glare means they must immediately stop whatever it is they are doing.

I don't believe in pinning a puppy. It is unnecessary and if done incorrectly, can have adverse repercussions.

I will use anything available to me for bribing. Some of my favourite foods to use are peanut butter, cheese spread, cheese pieces, wieners, and liver or beef heart. Peanut butter and cheese spread are great for puppies to lick as it takes longer to lick it off the table or other object than it takes to eat a bit of liver. However, you can rub meat and cheese to leave a film to keep a puppy busy. Bits of meat or cheese work well to get the puppy to follow the food to manipulate him into a position. The easiest way to remember how to use food with puppies is that wherever the nose goes, the rest of the body will follow. Holding the food slightly above the nose will cause the nose to go up and the butt to go down into a sit. Holding the food in front of the nose and moving it away will cause the puppy to move forward into a standing position. For wild puppies, a squeaky toy or ball to chew on works just as well as food.

Meet and greet the puppy

The puppy will come into your shop either on a leash or being held by the owner. Our first reaction to a puppy is to coo and ahh over him. However, it is best to ignore the puppy and resist the urge to reach out and snap it away from the owner. Tell the owners he's cute and sweet, because he is, but avoid handling and mauling as soon as he enters your shop. The puppy is already unsure of the situation. He is not quite settled in his new home and has had a lot of changes in the past few weeks. If the puppy is in the owner's arms, check if the puppy has a leash and/or collar on. Put on a light-weight shop leash and a small shop collar or harness if needed. Ask the owner to put the puppy on the floor to investigate the area. Yes, he'll probably urinate. While the puppy is investigating, take the information from the owner about the puppy for your records. By allowing the puppy to investigate at his own pace, he can get comfortable and feel safe. If paid a lot of attention to, it could set the puppy on edge rather than put him at ease. Some puppies will relish attention, while others will not.

After all the information is taken, explain to the owner exactly what is going to be done to the puppy at this visit and stress that you will need the puppy for at least three to four hours. Time always depends on the puppy, the breed, and where he came from. By explaining to the owner the steps you will be taking and what the puppy will be learning, you also make the owner feel safe. Owners of new puppies are very worried about leaving their puppy in an environment that they themselves are unsure of. It is the groomer's responsibility to make the owners feel safe.

Ask the obvious questions: Are vaccinations up to date? Are there any medical problems? Where did the puppy come from? Is anyone in the house allergic to peanuts? (Important if using peanut butter in the training procedure.)

At this point, hold the leash and tell the owner you will call them when the puppy is done. Allow the puppy to watch the owner leave. You can expect at least one phone call from the owner during the session asking how the puppy is doing. Some owners may insist on staying. If you're comfortable with it, let them stay, but tell them that if you feel pressured or you feel they are raising unnecessary anxiety in the shop, you will ask them to leave. The first visit is the only visit in the three-part puppy program that I will allow the owner to stay.

At the age between 12 to 15 weeks, the puppy has not yet established a solid bond with the owner. During the grooming session, the puppy will not be entirely focused on the owner; therefore, this session is relatively easy with the owner present.

Let's groom

The owner has left and it's just you and the puppy. You have two choices: you can put the puppy in a cage or crate or let him wander around. If you let him wander around, make sure there are no other dogs loose that could harm or scare the puppy. If you have another puppy around the same age and size, check with both owners to be sure the puppies can play together before the bath. I always try to book in two puppies at the same time so they can play and tire each other out. The grooming shop becomes something fun, rather than a place to be fearful of. However, if you have a boisterous puppy and a fearful puppy, always monitor their play and separate them if it looks like one puppy is getting overwhelmed. Always book puppies with calm experienced dogs in the shop. By working on another dog, the puppy can watch and learn that there is nothing to fear. The puppy also gets exposed to the sound of the equipment from a distance, which is advantageous for sound sensitive dogs. Sight sensitive dogs will be exposed to moving objects, which will prepare them when it's their turn.

While the puppy is either in the cage or wandering around, clean the table and put all the equipment you will be introducing to the puppy on it.

Equipment needed is:

> thinning shears
> straight edge shears
> clippers
> pin brush
> slicker brush
> nail clippers
> comb
> flea comb
> treats

Ready for puppy?

Sit on the floor and call the puppy to you whether he is on the floor or in the crate. Be happy, but not overwhelming. Some puppies will come running to you, jump in your lap, and snuggle in. Cradle the puppy in your arms, stand up and move the puppy to the table.

Sounds easy, right? But what if the puppy runs partway to you and runs away? Or what if he just runs from you or he won't even come out of the cage? Remember the leash you put on when the owner was there—the leash that you haven't taken off, yet? Hold the leash and call the puppy again. Coax him to you with your voice and treats, all the while gently pulling the leash so the puppy is coming to you. Avoid smiling a big toothy smile as it can indicate that you are going to eat the puppy. The puppy will struggle, but be calm, soothing and quiet. When the puppy is within reaching distance, do not make a grab for puppy. Let the puppy come closer to you, close enough that you can slip you hand under the chest and gently lift the puppy into your lap. Hold the puppy against your chest so he can feel your heart beat. Stand up with the puppy and move him to the table.

Gently put the puppy on the table while saying *Table*. Every time you put the puppy on the table, say the word *Table*; this is training the puppy to associate the word table with a grooming table. Always keep a hand on the puppy or a finger in the collar to prevent the puppy from leaping or falling off the table.

If you use a noose, put the noose on whenever the puppy is on the table. When attaching the noose to the grooming arm, lower the arm so the puppy has lots of slack to move around. Do not noose the puppy so he's strung up by his neck—the puppy will panic. Never leave a puppy noosed and on the table—he can fall off and hang itself. Never leave the puppy loose on the table and walk away. Always have a hold of the collar with your hand.

Sit so you aren't towering over the puppy.

Let the puppy walk around the table and sniff the equipment you have placed there. Place some small treats in amongst the equipment for the puppy to find.

Gently put a hand on each side and stop the puppy. Say *Stop* in a soft but firm voice.

When the puppy freezes, praise him. Repeat this two to three times. This is the beginning of teaching the word *Stop*, which means to stop moving.

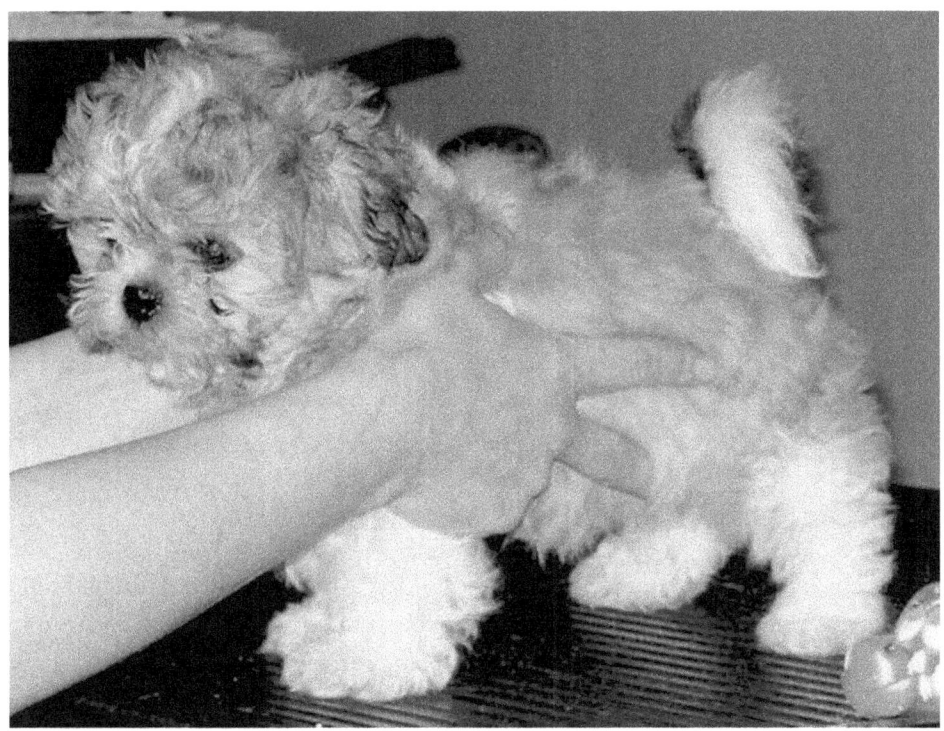

Gently put a finger or your hand under the flank and say *Stand*, gently lifting the puppy into a stand position if needed. Repeat two to three times.

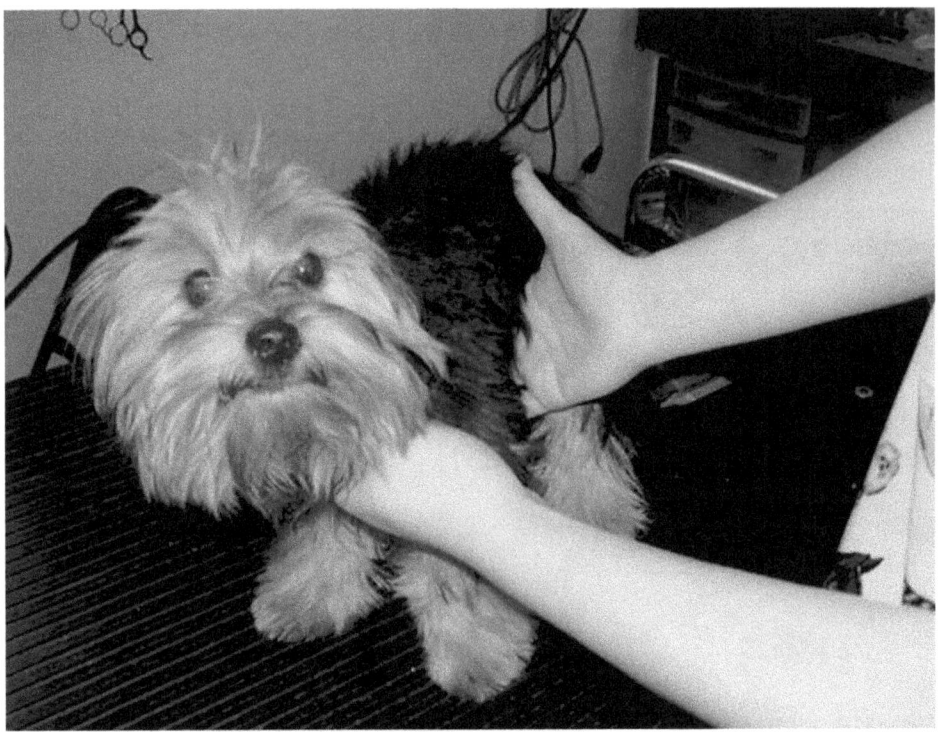

Now you have added another command and the puppy will learn that *Stand* means to stand and *Stop* means to stop moving. Whenever you move the puppy into a new position that he needs to be standing for, put a finger under the flank and say *Stand*. If puppy starts to sit, slip you finger under his flank and tell him to *Stand*. Couple the *Stand* command with the *Stop* command. For example, *Stand*, hand under the flank, then *Stop*. Always praise when he has done something you've asked him to do. Even if it isn't perfect, praise him.

Touch and feel
Starting at the muzzle, stroke the face going with the grain of the hair, stroke the cheeks, head, ears (inside and outside of the ear), neck, throat, shoulder, each front leg, picking up each foot and stroking between the toes, the back, sides, hips, back legs, back toes, tail, and rear. When you get to the tail, lift the tail up, all the time praising the puppy and repeating the *Stand* and *Stop* commands and exercises. This method of petting or stroking mimics the way a bitch would groom her puppies. It is very soothing and relaxing for the puppy as well as indicating where he is touchy.

After you are done stroking, gently repeat the *Stop* exercise twice. Take the puppy off the table, sit on the floor and give the puppy a play for a minute or two. Then bring the puppy back on the table. You don't have to sit on the floor with the puppy, you can let him walk around on the floor, chase some toys, or play with another puppy if you have one in the shop. Taking him off the table teaches him that on the table it's grooming time and on the floor it's break time.

Positions
Warning—when teaching the different positions to the puppy, don't lift or pull the legs too high or too far. The shoulders and hips can be injured easily if they are over extended.

Starting at the head, hold the head in different positions, mimicking positions you'll need to hold the head when styling. Lift the lips to look at the teeth. Run your fingers on the upper and lower gums.

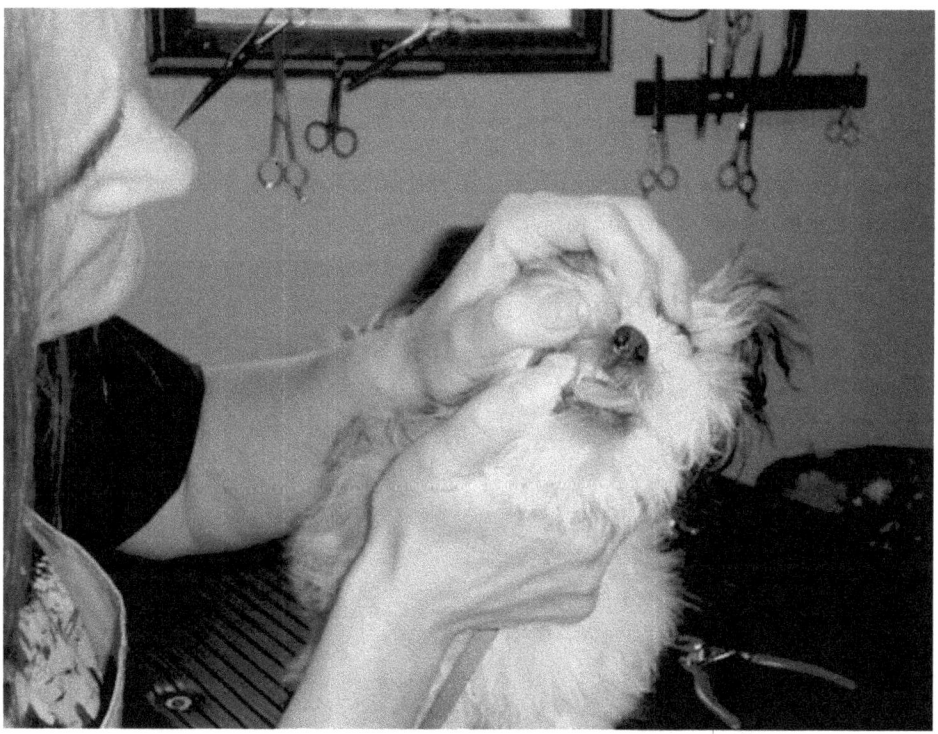

Whenever the puppy fidgets with each new thing, tell him to *Stop*. Praise him when he stops.

Stroke each ear, flipping back the ear flap to look in the ear and give it a sniff.

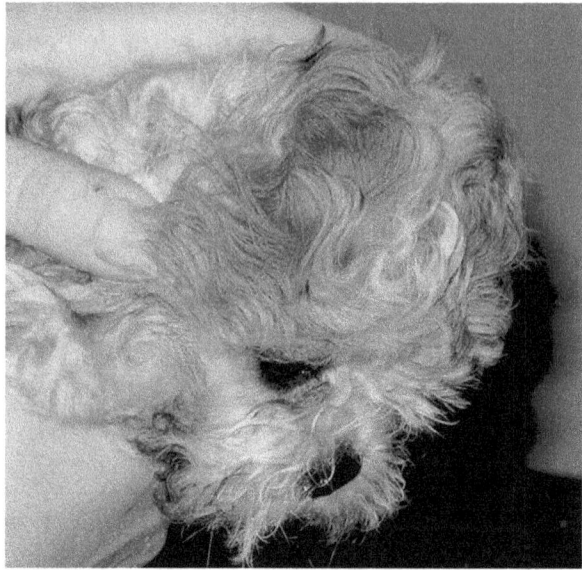

Run your hands down the shoulder to the left front leg.

Pick up the leg from the front and gently extend it, hold for one to two seconds, and then put it back it on the table.

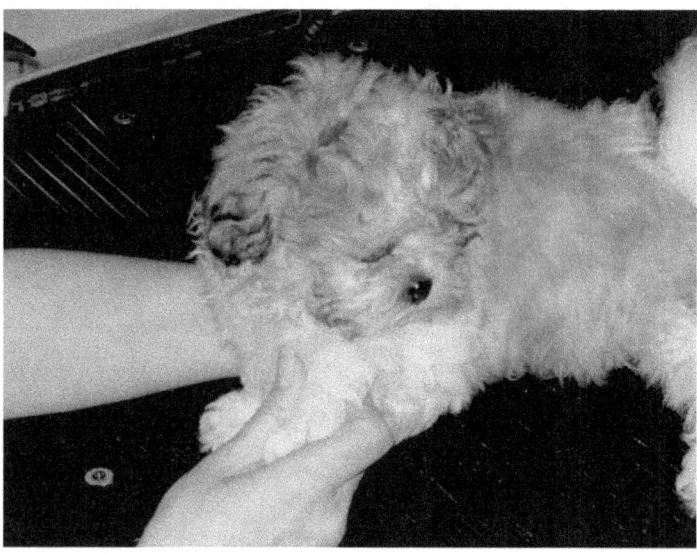

Pick up the left front leg again, but more off to the side as if you are going to shave under the leg. Rub the armpits with your finger. Put the front leg back where it was. Tell the puppy to *Stop* each time you lift a leg or change a position, and then praise him when he stops moving.

Move to the rear left leg. Lift it up as if you are tucking it under the puppy, hold it for one to two seconds, and put the leg back on the table. Lift it to the side as if you are shaving the inside of the thigh, run your hand along the inside of the thigh.

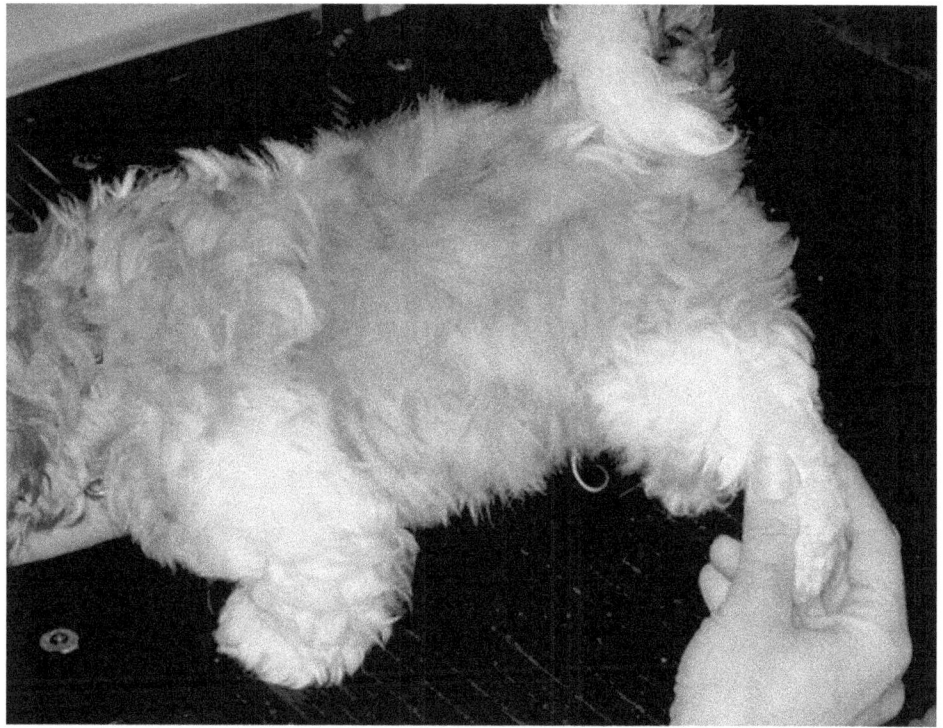

Put the leg back on the table. Lift the leg up and extend it to the rear of the puppy. Put it back on the table.

Move to the rear of the puppy. Pick up the puppy and move him into correct positions if you have to.

Lift the tail and touch the puppy underneath of tail, around the anus area, the pelvic area, and where the vulva or testicles are.

From the anus, move to rear left leg. Repeat the process as in the right rear leg.

Move up to the front right leg and repeat the process you did for the left front leg.

Go back to the head and face and run your fingers along the cheeks, in the eye crevasses, and around the ears. Put the puppy on the floor for some play time.

Bring the puppy back on the table.

Note—this is how I groom every dog or puppy. I start at the left front leg and work my way around. I style the head last. If you have a different routine, do the above exercises in the routine you typically use. By using a routine, the dog knows what to expect.

Equipment
Show the puppy a pin brush, let the puppy sniff it, lick it, and give it a chew.

Take the pin brush and run it over the puppy, starting with the legs and chest, the throat, around the side to the neck, and then continue on down the back. Praise the puppy the whole time.

Show the puppy a slicker brush, letting him sniff, lick, and chew it and then repeat the process above.

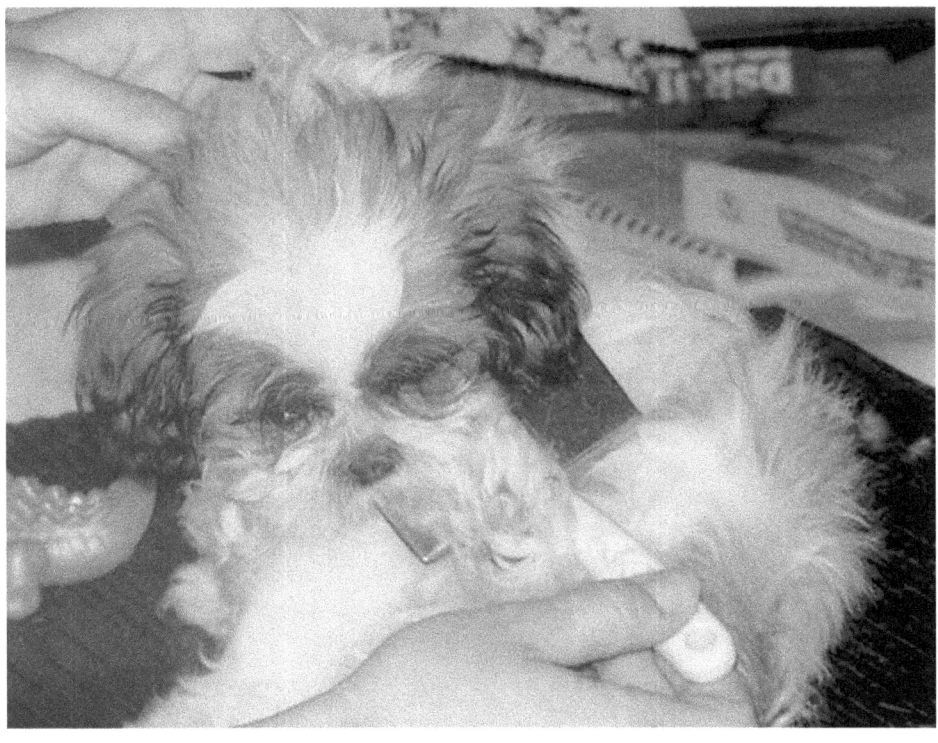

Next, do the same thing with a comb.

This process lets the puppy investigate different pieces of equipment through sight, smell, taste, and touch. The equipment after being thoroughly investigated, it becomes less intimidating and scary.

Secure thinning shears closed with either a piece of tape or elastic you use for bows. If you don't have thinning shears, use regular scissors, but only if they have a rounded or blunted end.

Again, let the puppy sniff, lick, and chew on shears.

While shears are closed, run them all over the body. When the puppy accepts this, gently hold the face and run the shears along the cheeks. Start at the base of the ear and run them against the ear. Move shears halfway down the cheek towards the muzzle and then run them with the grain of the hair to the ear.

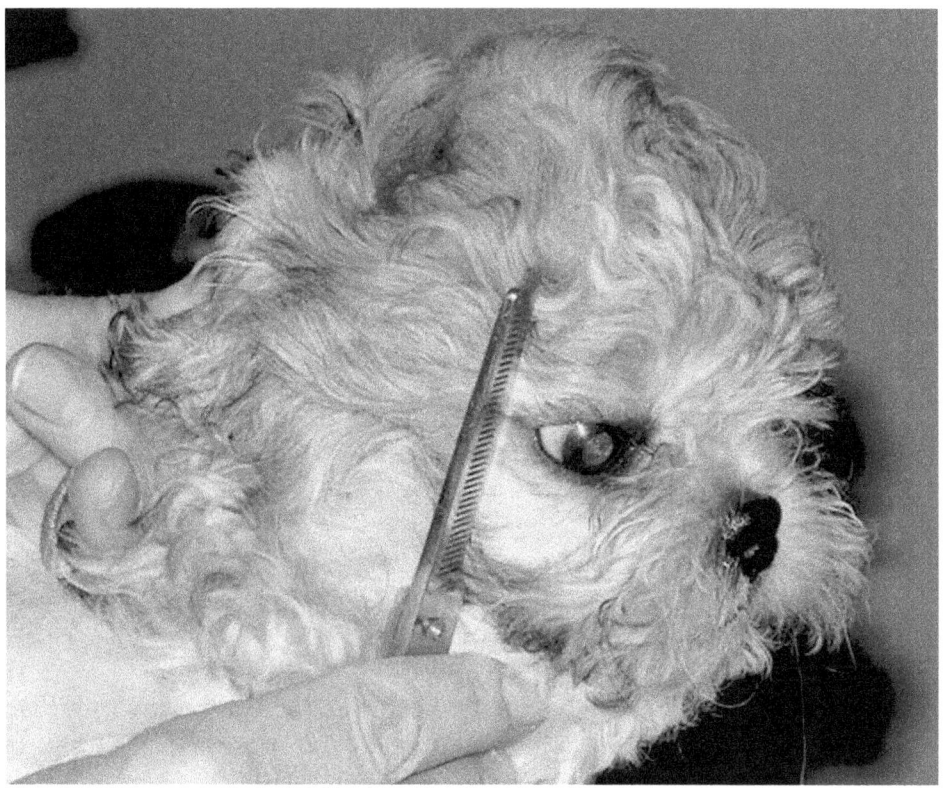

Gradually move the shears forward on the face until you get to the nose and run them back to the ear.

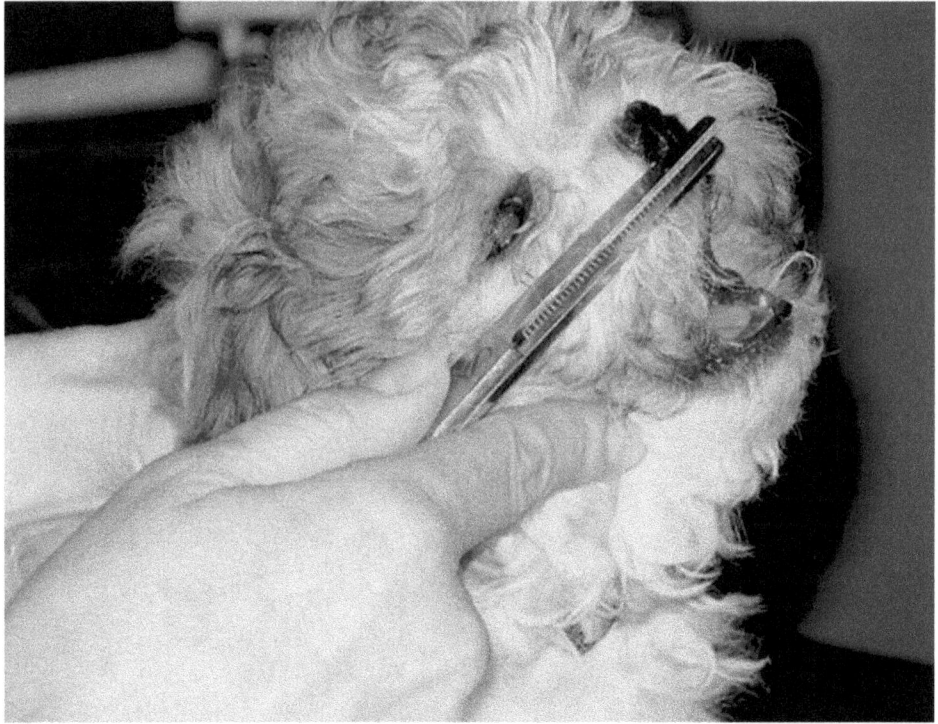

Do one side of the face first and then the other. If the puppy tries to bite at the shears, pause and then let him bite the shears. It won't take long for him to realize that shears aren't the best thing to chew. Always keep shears secured shut for this exercise. If you have open shears or scissors, you risk cutting the puppy.

When he is comfortable with the shears on his face, move up to the head. I suggest starting at the back of the head and working your way forward to the stop, rubbing the scissors in the direction of the fur. If you start at the stop (the forehead of the puppy) or above the eyes, the puppy will lift his head to follow the shears backward.

Hold his head steady and rub the shears in the crevasse of each eye.

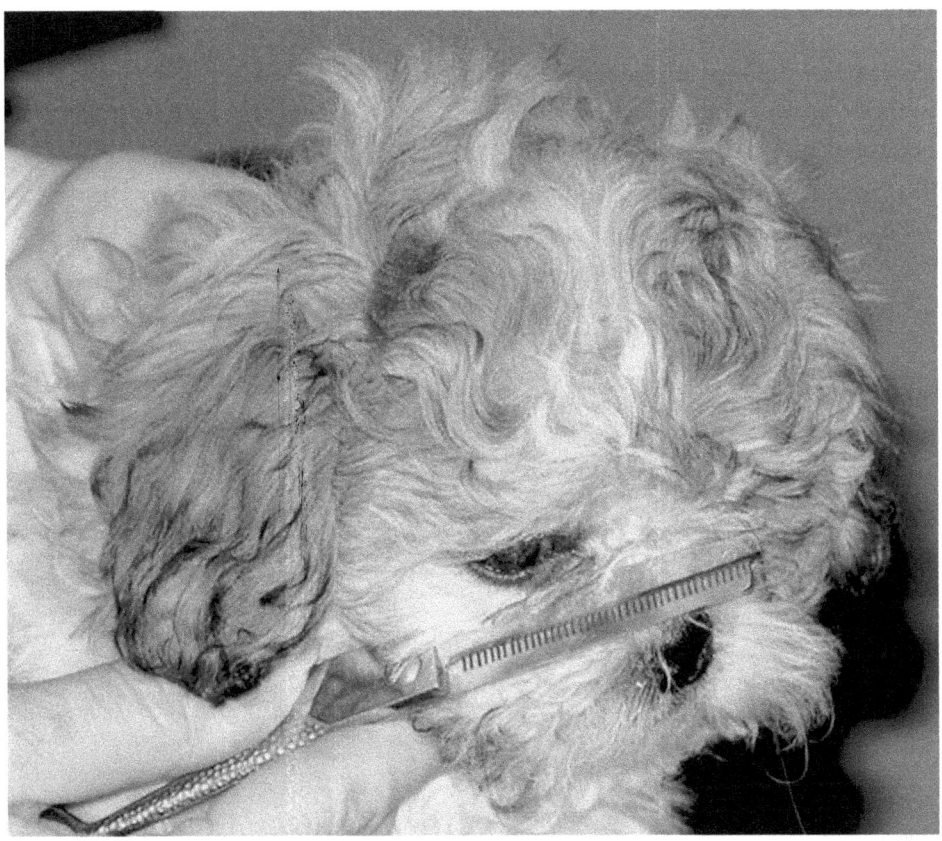

Allow the puppy move his head around. Don't clamp his head in a death grip. The puppy will show either no resistance or will fight against the feel of something foreign around his eyes. Let him get comfortable with the feel. Do not scissor the hair around the eyes at this stage, you are just getting the puppy accustomed to the feeling of something rubbing around the eyes in a safe manner.

Take a flea comb and gently comb the hair around the eyes. If there is a build-up of debris, wait until the bath before you comb around the eyes.

Now we introduce the sound of shears. Holding the thinning shears off the side about two inches away from the head, open and close them. Let the puppy sniff the shears again. When the puppy is satisfied with the shears, open and close them again. Do it over and over, eventually increasing the speed and the number of times you open and close them. When the puppy is comfortable with the sound, he will ignore it. While opening and closing the shears, move them around the body as if you were styling with them, keeping them about two inches away from the body.

Switch shears to a straight edge pair of scissors and repeat the process. Remember to use a pair of straight edge scissors with a blunt end.

Pick up the clippers, let the puppy sniff them, and run the clippers over the body without turning them on. Run them so blade is backwards to prevent any hair being pulled.

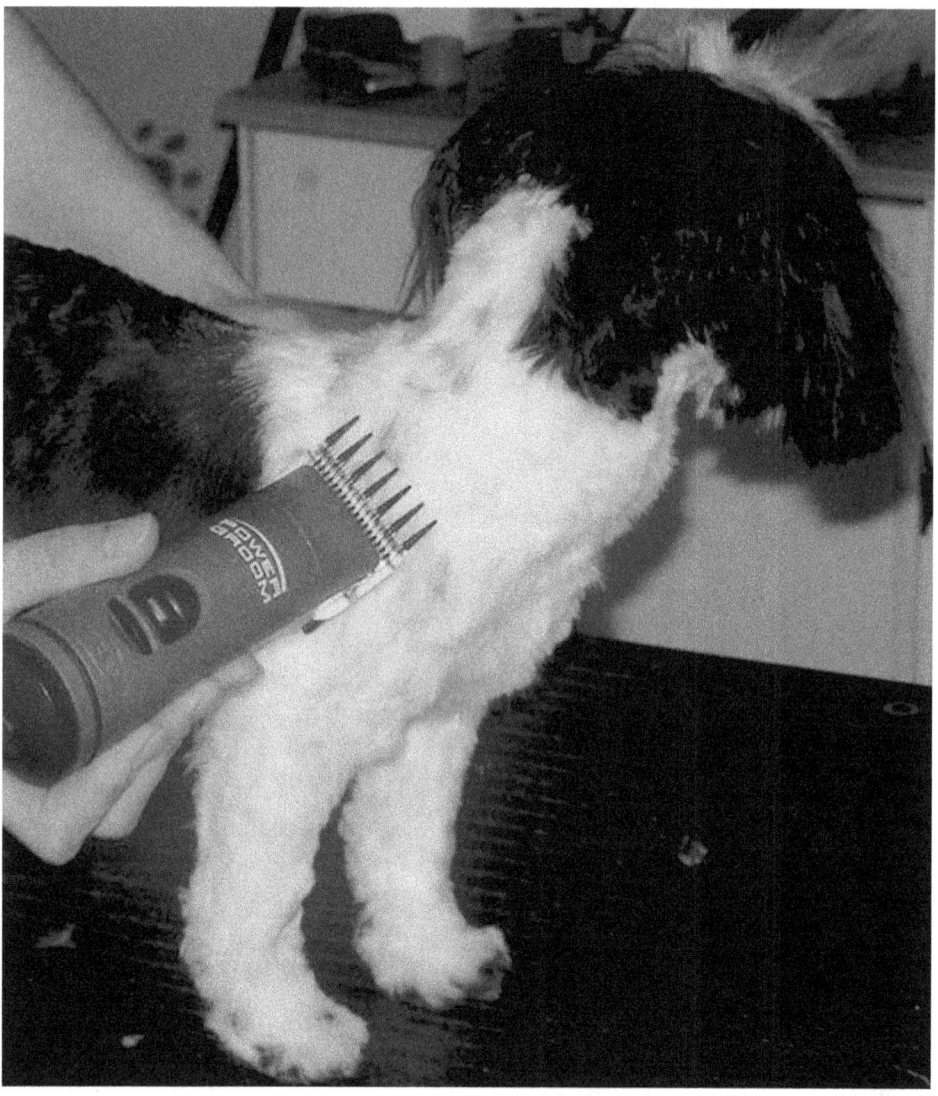

Hold the clippers away from the puppy and turn them on. Do not use clippers on the puppy; you are only exposing him to the sound. Move the clippers around the body, holding them about two to three inches away from the body.

Put the puppy on the floor for a play.

Pre-bath
Nails
Sit in a chair with the puppy in your lap. With one hand holding the puppy, pick up the toenail clippers.

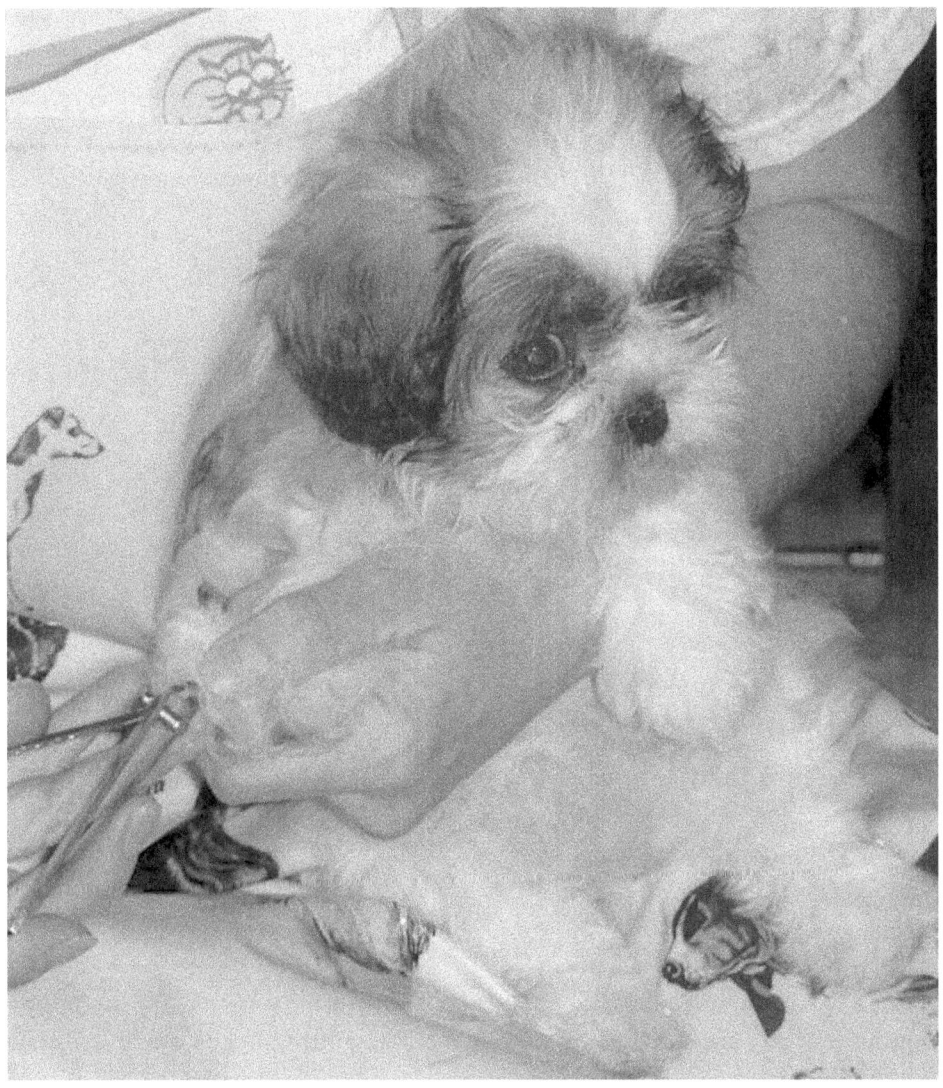

For the nails at this stage, I suggest using a pair of human toenail clippers. Hold the leg with your hand and gently spread the toes with your fingers and clip each nail.

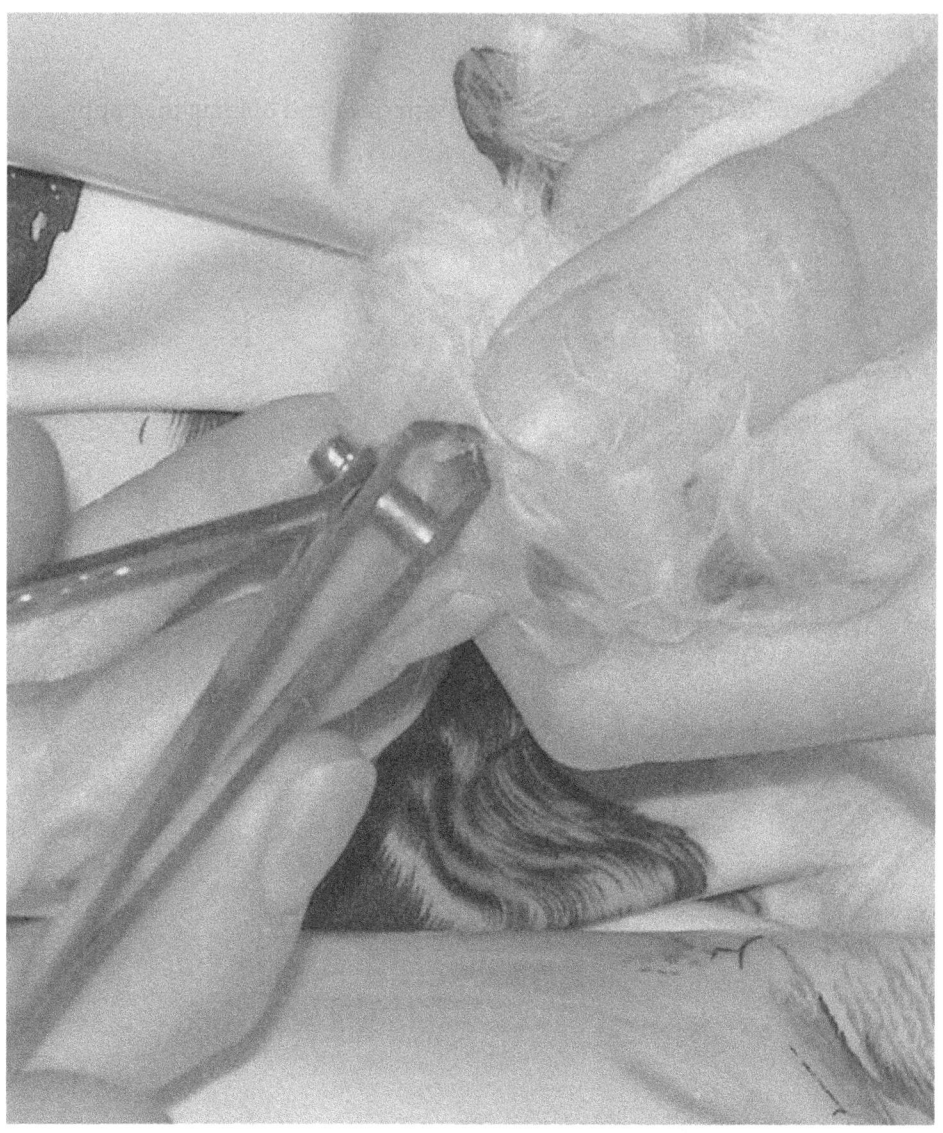

Don't be in a hurry to do this. Praise the puppy after each nail. If the puppy doesn't need it's nails cut, pretend to do them, going through the motions without actually cutting the nail.

Put the puppy on the table and give it a bit of a play.

Ear plucking
There is some controversy in the grooming industry as to whether plucking the ear hair is beneficial to the dog or not. Ear hairs act as a filter, preventing excess dirt and debris from entering the ear canal. Wax and debris can attach to the hair in the ears and get worked up and out of the ear. This is why the hair in the ears can be quite difficult to grip as it is coated with wax from the ear canal. Without the hair, the wax and debris builds up in the ear canal and on the walls of the ears, making it very difficult to clean. Many breeds have a tuft of hair at the opening of the ear canal. This tuft also acts as a filter to protect the ear canal.

An ear infection, in an ear with a build-up of hair, is very difficult to get under control as the hair, mixed with infection debris blocks much of the needed antibiotics. However, only a veterinarian should pluck an infected ear. An infected ear presents itself as red and hot with excess wax build-up clumping onto the ear hair. It is also itchy, smelly, and generally painful. The last thing the dog wants is to have the hair plucked out of an already tender ear. If unsure if the ear is infected, err on the side of caution—don't pluck the ears, send the pup to the vet. Puppies will often come in with ear mites, microscopic bugs in the ear that live by sucking blood from the walls of the ear canal. Ear mites will often present the same way as an ear infection, so send the pup to the vet. Ear mites can transfer dog to dog through ear pluckers.

This being said, it is your choice whether to pluck or not. I have many dogs that I don't pluck the hair and I have many dogs that I do. Whether or not I pluck the ears depends on the owner and the individual dog. Some dogs are very uncomfortable when the hair in their ears gets too long and will start scratching. Some dogs are a menace when it comes to ear plucking.

If you choose not to pluck, always clean the ears with a specialized cleaner meant for dog ears. I like to comb the hair in the ears to prevent matting within the ear canal. If I have a dog with an excess of hair in the ears, I will often simply pluck half the hair rather than the full ear and only pluck the hair that comes out easily.

Whether you pluck ears or not, I feel that puppies should be accustomed to the feeling of a few hairs being plucked out in case later on in life they grow into a dog that needs repeated ear plucking.

Tell the puppy to *Stop*. Lift an ear—it doesn't matter whether it is the right or left. If you use ear powder, let the puppy smell and taste the bottle. Sprinkle a bit in the ear or sprinkle a bit on your fingers. Ear powder is not meant to fill the ear canal and can cause ear infections if used improperly. Use just enough to dust the hairs with powder, this will coat the hair enough to give you a better grip on the hair.

Gently pull out one or two hairs at a time with your fingers.

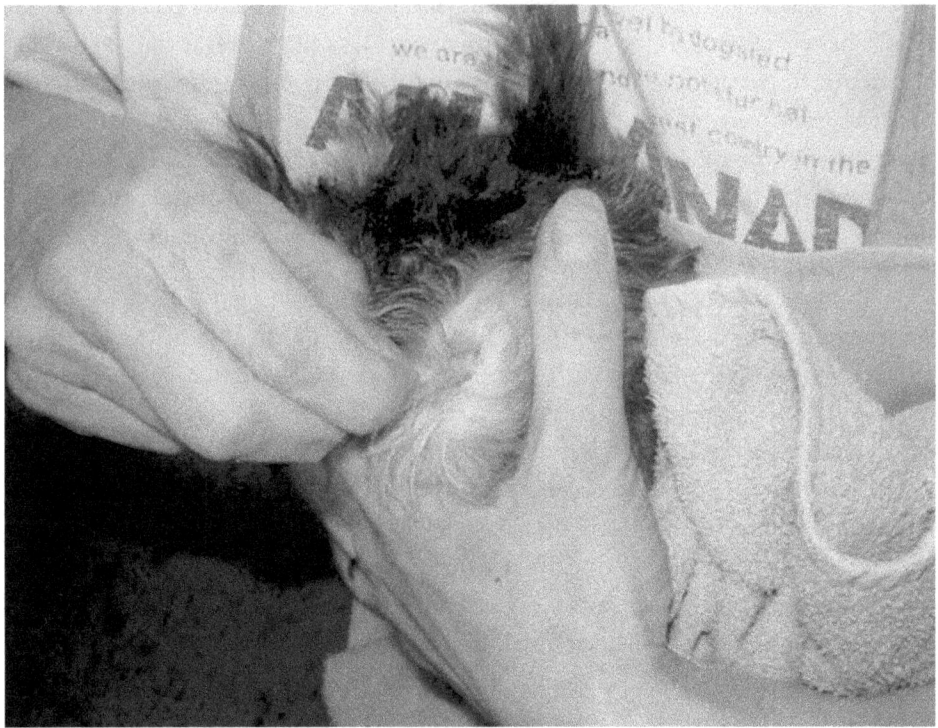

Soak a cotton ball or cotton pad with ear cleaner and wipe out any debris in the ear. If you have a puppy that doesn't need his ears plucked, just clean the ears. When ears are plucked and cleaned, set the puppy on the floor and get the bath ready.

What to expect
The puppy will move a lot, especially when you are touching him and moving his legs into unnatural positions. The key here is to go at the pace of the puppy. Don't yell or scream or get into a tug of war with his legs. You're holding his legs in different grooming positions in a quiet, safe manner. If he struggles, do the exercise a few times until he realizes you aren't killing him, you're just holding his body parts in different positions. This is a gradual way to introduce the grooming process and to allow the puppy to get comfortable with different holds and positions before you try to use the scissors or clippers. Once he is used to you holding his legs, face, and ears and touching his body in a non-threatening way, it is easy to introduce different pieces of equipment without overwhelming him. It is normal for puppies to twist around every time you introduce a new piece of equipment or a new position. Let him see what you are doing and investigate. He already knows what the brush is from playing with it on the table. He will be

curious about it again when you start brushing him with it, but will settle much easier than if you picked up a brush and started brushing him without letting him investigate it first.

Troubleshooting table work

You will get some puppies that will panic every time you do something new. Take a bit of extra time with these puppies. They may need time to adjust to new stimuli.

Legs: Run your hand from shoulder to leg, pause, and then lift the leg. This gives the puppy a bit more time to adjust to the new sensation and to accept that it isn't hurtful.

Face: Hold the face, pause, and then move it into a different position.

Brush: Put brush on puppy, pause, and then take one stroke. Pause, and then take another.

Do you see a pattern? Scared, cautious and tough guy puppies need a moment to adjust to new stimuli. Always pause and always move your hands over the puppy towards the body part you need to work with rather than going straight for the part. For example, move your hand down the shoulder to the leg, rather than picking the leg up right away.

Nails: The nice thing about puppies is they are easily distracted with food. Peanut butter is great choice as it can be smeared on the table or on your arm and it takes a bit of work for the puppy to lick it off, thereby distracting him for a longer period of time than a piece of food would. I always check with the owner to confirm there are no peanut allergies at home and can use a cheese spread instead of peanut butter. Use peanut butter or cheese spread before the bath, as it can get messy around the mouth. With the puppy in your lap, smear some peanut butter on the side of the table so the puppy can lick it off while you are clipping the nails.

You can also spread it on your arm that is holding the puppy, so he can lick it off your arm and you are keeping him in a more secure position.

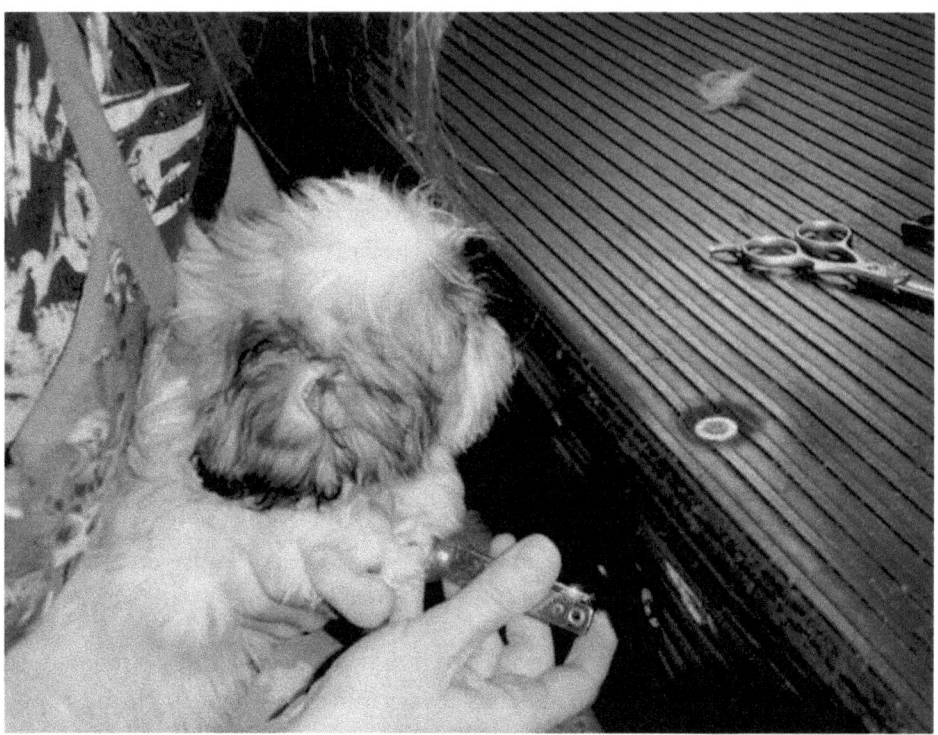

If food isn't working as a distraction, stand with puppy in your arms, holding a foot out with one hand and clipping the nails with another. If the puppy squirms in your arms, simply relax your arm so the puppy suddenly drops a bit. Do not drop puppy, you're just fake dropping him. This will usually settle him down if you do this a few times. Accompany the word *Stop* whenever you want him to stop moving.

After the bath, when the puppy is wrapped in a towel and held in your arms, is also a good time to cut the nails. They are so concerned with being wet that they rarely notice you cutting their nails.

Ear plucking: The trick with ear plucking is to pluck one or two hairs at a time. Finger plucking is more appeasing at this stage. Often, it will be easier if you wait until you are doing the finishing on the puppy, roll him in a towel like a sausage with his head sticking out, and pluck the ears with him cradled in your arms. If you use an ear plucking tool, you run the risk of hurting the ear with the tool. If you have a puppy that is getting aggressive about the ear plucking, stop and get the owners to pluck the ears at home over the next 4 weeks. (See homework for owners.)

The bath
Always tether a puppy in the tub.

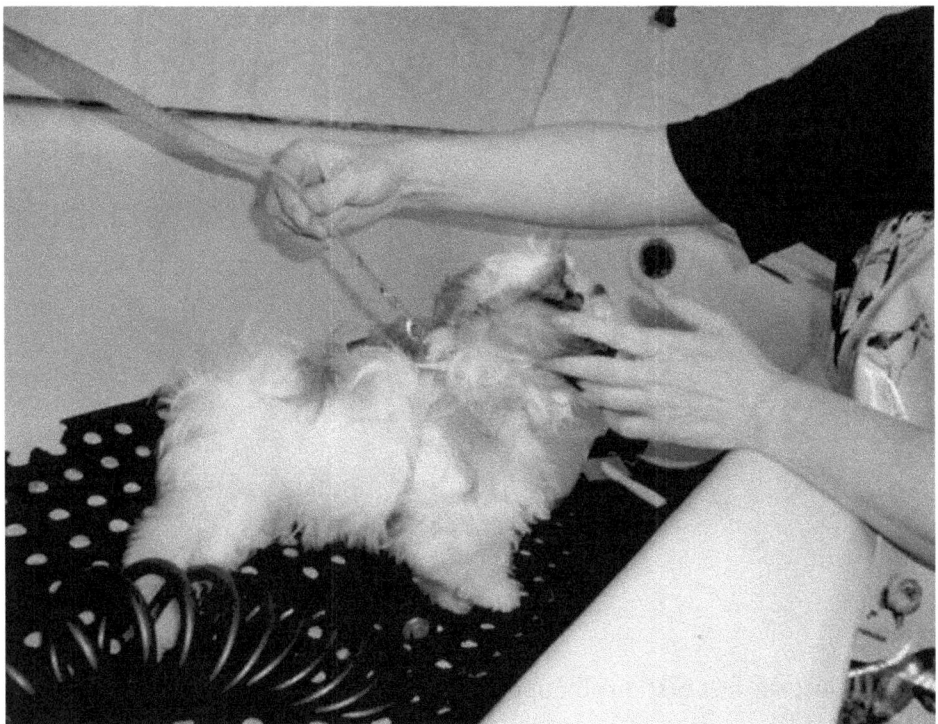

Puppies can and will jump around, possibly jumping out of tub which could result in a broken leg or neck. I always have a shop collar or harness on the puppy and prefer to use a harness on puppies, unless they are giant breeds and I don't have a harness big enough for them. You can also use a halti, which prevents pressure on the throat.

Make sure you have all the soap, conditioner, and equipment ready for the bath. Put the puppy in the tub and give him a minute to sniff around. Run the water and let the puppy see the water coming out of the hose.

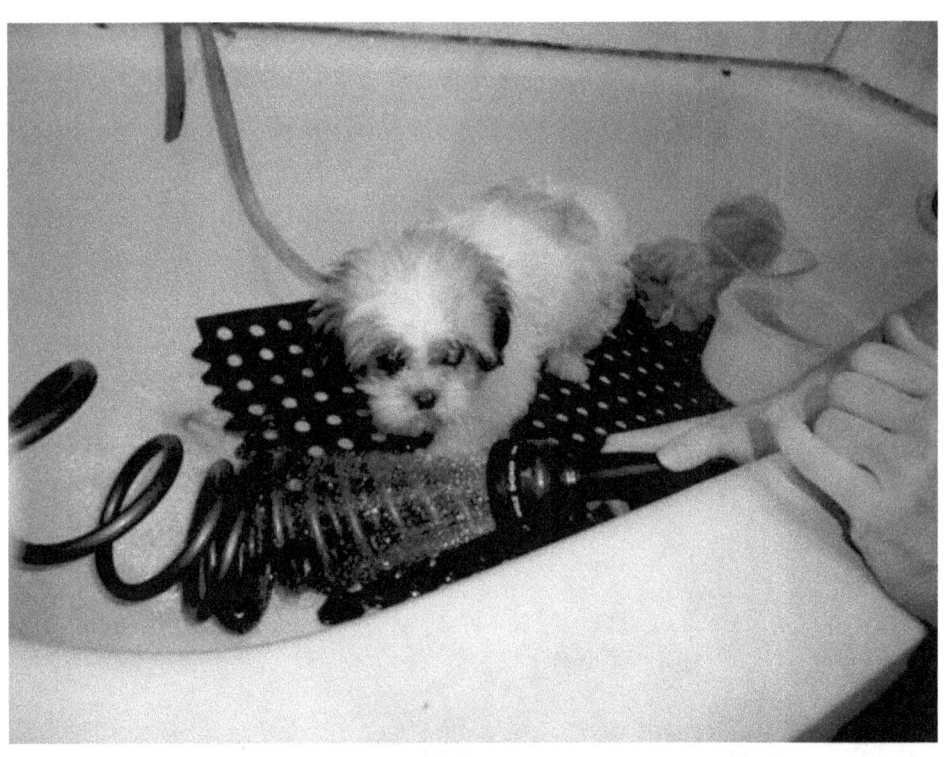

I always wet the feet first on all puppies and dogs.

This lessens the surprise of the water on their back. Get the feet wet and work upwards on the legs, ribs, chest and back to completely wet the puppy. I don't wet the head at this point. Shampoo thoroughly. When rinsing, again get the feet wet with the hose, and then move up to the back. Start a thorough rinse from neck and back down to the feet. Before the second shampoo, put cotton balls in the ears to prevent water from entering the ear canal, put the hose against the skull starting at the back of the head, working the hose over the head and cheeks, forcing the water to pour down the face and muzzle. Hold the muzzle down with the nose pointing to the floor of the tub to prevent water from getting in the nose. Dogs and puppies hate getting water sprayed in their face. Shampoo the whole puppy and scrub the feet well. Before rinsing, use a flea comb to remove any debris that may have collected in the corners of the eyes. If there is no debris, comb the hair with the flea comb as if you were combing out debris. Allowing the build-up of debris to soak in the tub makes it easier to comb it out.

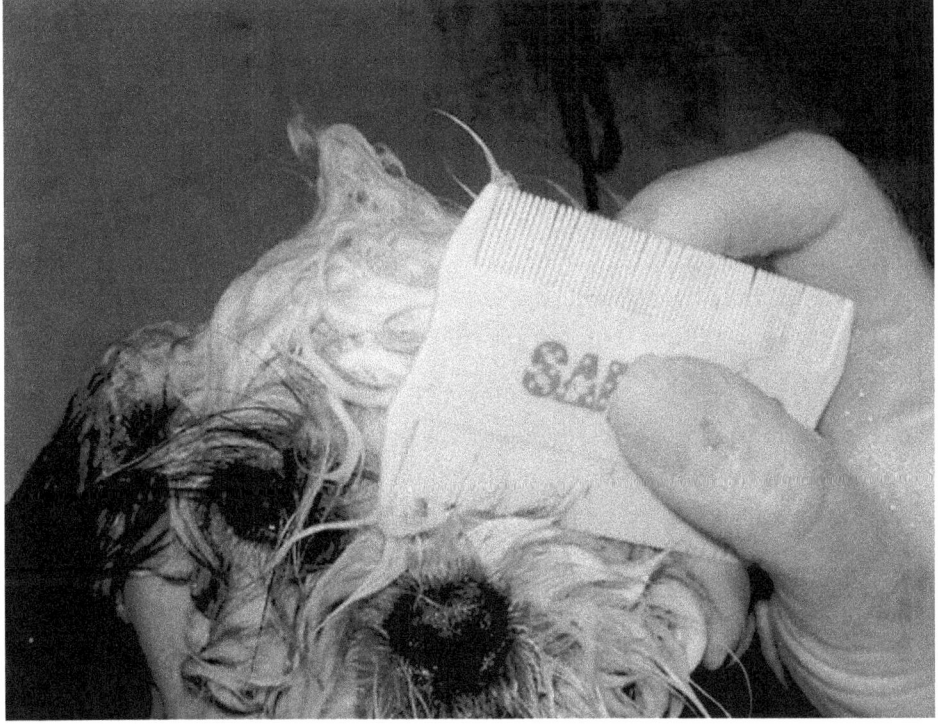

Replace the cotton balls in the ears if the puppy has shaken them out, and rinse and condition as you normally would, always spraying the feet first to give the puppy warning that the spray is coming.

When the puppy is thoroughly rinsed, towel dry and hold the puppy in your arms for a bit. This is the perfect time to cut the nails if you were having trouble before. This has been quite a lot for the puppy to deal with and he will need a bit of comfort. While he is in your arms, turn on the high voltage dryer for ten seconds if you have one, but hold the hose behind your back. You are introducing the puppy only to the noise. Place the puppy in a cage and turn on the cage dryer. I either have the cage dryer blowing to the floor of the cage or up top so the puppy gets the warmth, but air isn't blowing directly into his face. If you don't normally cage dry, I would strongly suggest that you cage dry him for a short amount of time so he is introduced to cage drying.

What to expect
Puppy's first bath will probably go like this:

The puppy goes in the tub. You tether the puppy in. The puppy pulls at the restrictive tether and starts to whine and cry. He tries to eat the tether to free himself.

You start the water; this takes the puppy's mind off the tether. He sniffs at the water and may even dunk his head in the spray. You start to wet the puppy at the feet. The puppy starts to panic and tries desperately to get away from the water. In order to prevent the puppy from hurting himself, you drop the hose and try to catch the puppy with both hands. But the puppy has become like a bird flying around on the tether in the tub. You finally catch the puppy. You try to reassure the puppy that it is only water. While holding the puppy, you retrieve the hose (which is hopefully in the tub), and you soak the puppy down. The puppy tries to claw his way up your arm to escape the water. You say a silent prayer that no clients are walking by to hear the screaming puppy

The bath sounds a lot easier on paper than in reality. For some puppies, this is their first bath. They may whine, cry, fight, and try everything in their power to jump out. Just keep reassuring them, telling them they are a good puppy, and get through it as fast and efficiently as possible. Always hold onto the collar or harness to minimize the puppy's movements.

The puppy will probably cry and whine in the cage with the dryer—ignore him. He will settle.

While the puppy is drying, work on another dog, preferably one that needs clipper work and a dog that is experienced at grooming and is calm. You don't want to work on a difficult dog around the puppy, he will get scared and worried if you are working on a growling or nervous dog.

When the puppy is dry or almost dry, take him from the cage, sit him on your lap and finish drying him by hand. If he is dry, use the cool setting on your dryer and fluff him out.

When cage drying, always have the setting on medium or low. Always have the puppy in a cage that is easily seen and can be monitored constantly. Puppies can overheat very quickly and can succumb to heat exhaustion rapidly.

Troubleshooting the bath

Stay calm. In my shop, we have different classifications for puppies and dogs in the tub: awesome, jumpers, rodeos, and lunatic. (We wear rain jackets with the lunatics).

For some puppies, I will hold them in one hand (they are still tethered in) and bath them with the other. Hum or sing if it will keep you calm and laugh. This may be the first bath the puppy has ever had and he is scared. Getting upset or mad won't help his fear. I would rather hold them in my hand than risk a neck injury or have them leaping from the tub. They remain tethered, just in my hand especially Yorkies and other tiny puppies.

For some puppies you can minimize their panic by rinsing the head with a glass of water to flush the shampoo, rather than spraying with the hose.

Have extra cotton balls for the ears ready as you will probably have to replace them before each rinse.

Finishing
The Body/legs/feet

Put the puppy on the floor to wander around while you get the table ready. You'll need:
- scissors
- thinning shears
- pin or slicker brush
- comb
- clippers

Put the puppy on the table, saying the word *Table*. Starting with the left front foot, trim the leg, pads, and foot with the scissors and/or thinning shears. Gently hold the front left leg so the elbow is at a right angle and scissor any stray hairs around the leg. Put the foot back on the table. Pick up the foot again and scissor the pads and the top of the foot. If you are styling a round foot, place the foot back on the table and scissor the foot in a round shape while the foot is on the table.

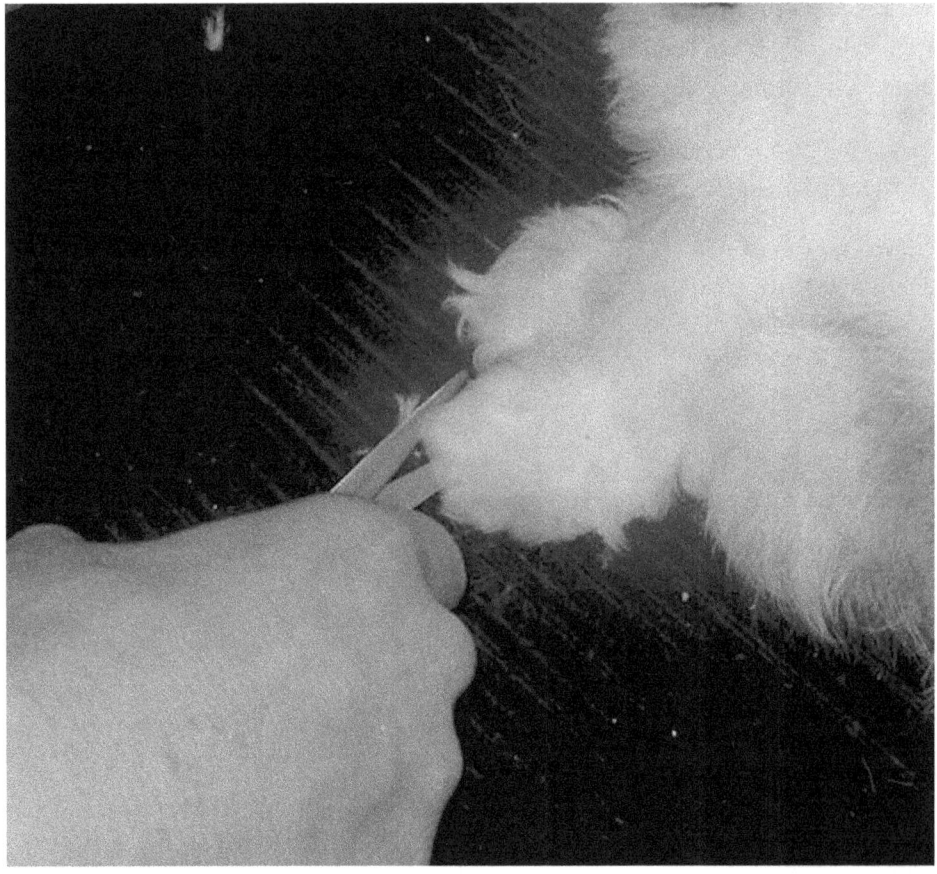

Trim the sides and back. Lift the left rear foot and extend it slightly towards the rear and scissor the leg. Place the foot back on the table, praise the puppy, and pick up the foot to scissor the pads and shape the foot.

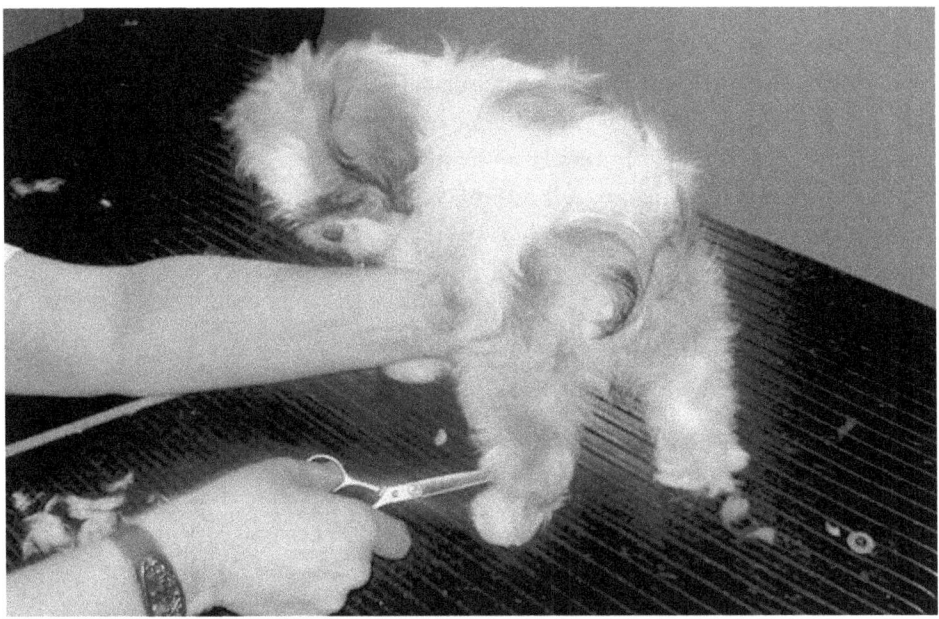

Shape the tail and scissor a poop chute or pee path.

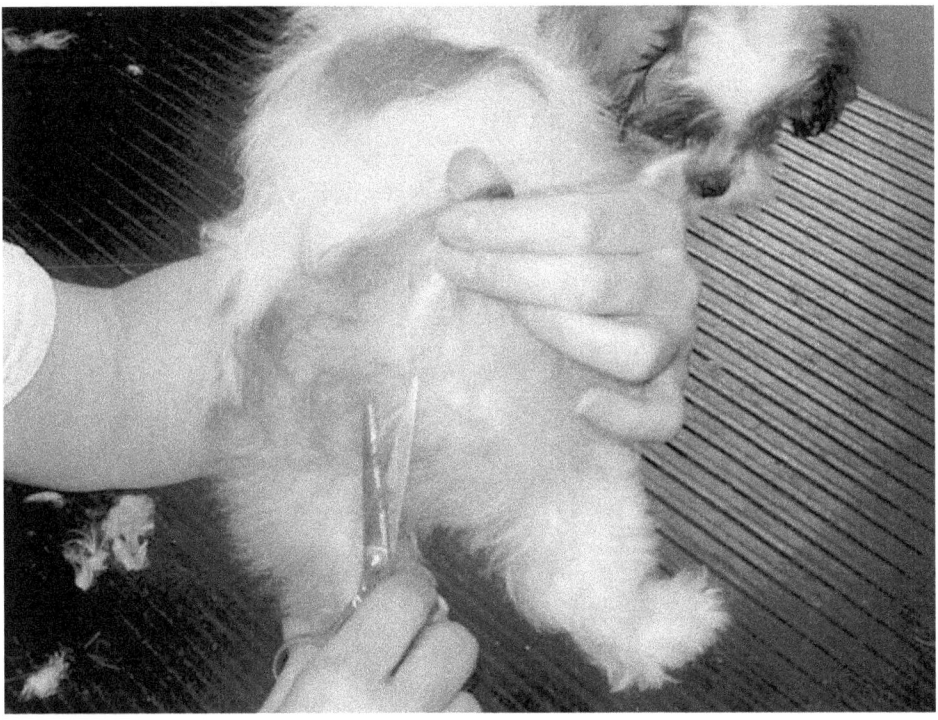

Carry on to the right side of the puppy finishing the rear leg, foot sides and front foot and leg as the left side. Scissor the armpits for each front leg. If you are wary about cutting the puppy with the scissors, comb the hair, but don't pull the comb all the way through the hair. Scissor the hair trapped in the teeth of the comb. The comb acts as a barrier between the scissors and skin to prevent an accidental cut. If the puppy wants to sit, let him sit to trim up the chest, throat, and neck area. The puppy is probably very tired by now and you may have to support him in a standing or sitting position. If puppy wants to lie down, let him lie down and scissor what you can while he's laying down.

If you have a Poodle or any puppy that requires shaved toes, shave each foot as you work your way around the puppy.

Face
There is nothing worse than having a Shih Tzu that you can't get near his face to groom. This is where all your patience and training come into play. With puppies, do the face and head last—they are tired and will either offer no fight or fight very little.

Starting with the back of the head, shape the head with thinning shears.

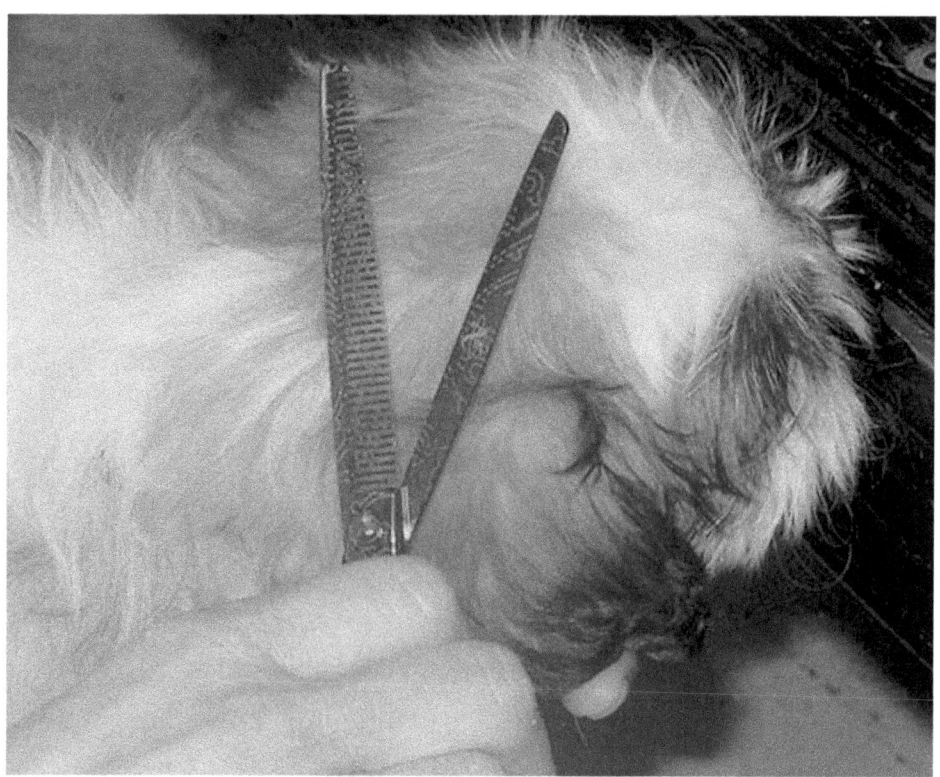

Thinning shears make a noise when you use them fast; this prepares the puppy for the clipper sound. If the puppy happens to jerk, you won't cut a big chunk of hair and have to spend extra time trying to even it out. You want to work from the back to the front of the head and face; the puppy will be less likely to tip his head back to follow the shears. For the cheeks, flip the ear back out of the way. Start scissoring from the ear and work to the front of the muzzle. Use the same process for the chin, start at the base of the throat and work forward to the chin.

The puppy has already experienced the sound and feel of the shears on his head before the bath, so this isn't such a shock and he will accept this much easier.

What to expect
Expect a bit of head flailing once you start cutting hair. Tell the puppy to *Stop* and cut, pause, cut, pause. Most puppies will settle.

Eyes
Save the eyes for last. Run the thinning shears along the corner of the eyes. Continue doing this until the puppy is relaxed. Open the thinning shears, gently rub the lower blade in the corner, under the hair growing there, Close the thinning shears and hold them there.

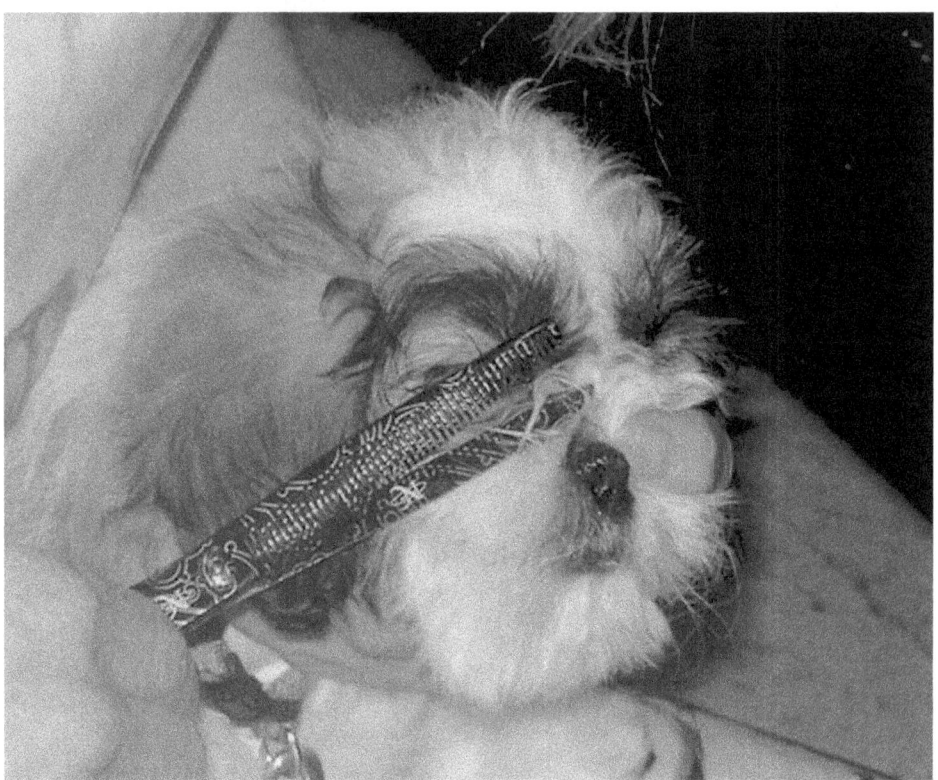

If puppy struggles, tell him to *Stop* and try to hold the thinning shears flush in the corner of the eye. When the puppy stops struggling, open and close thinning shears again. Pause and do it again and again until all the hair is trimmed. Move to the other eye. There are two ways to approach the other eye. You can slide the thinning shears over the nose so the end is pointing down and start scissoring the hair...

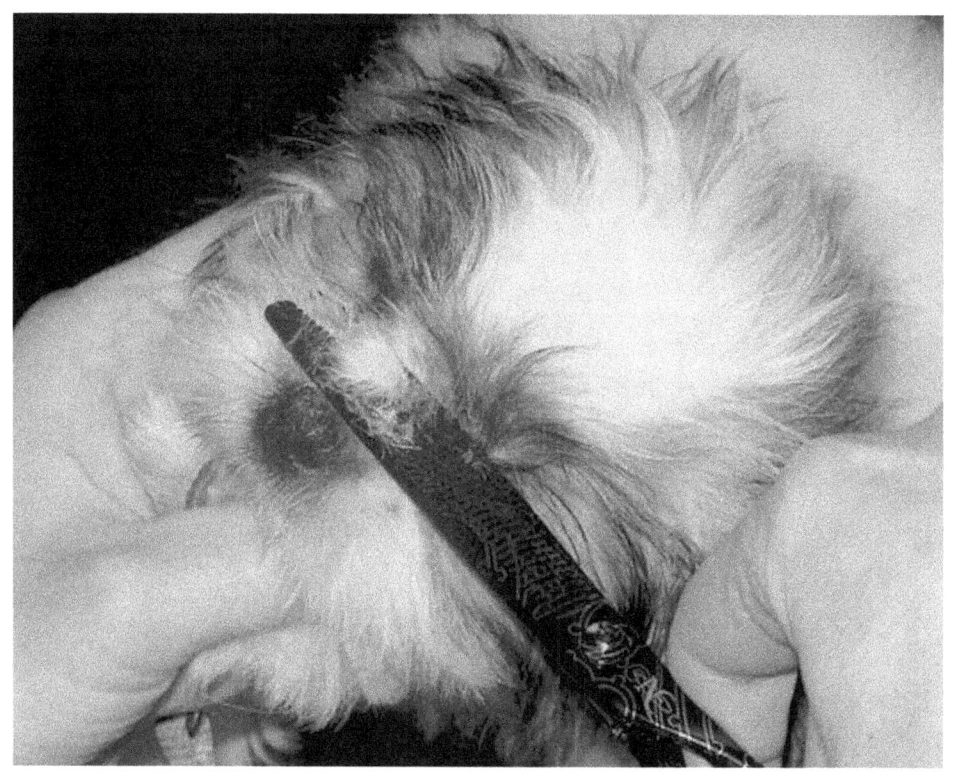
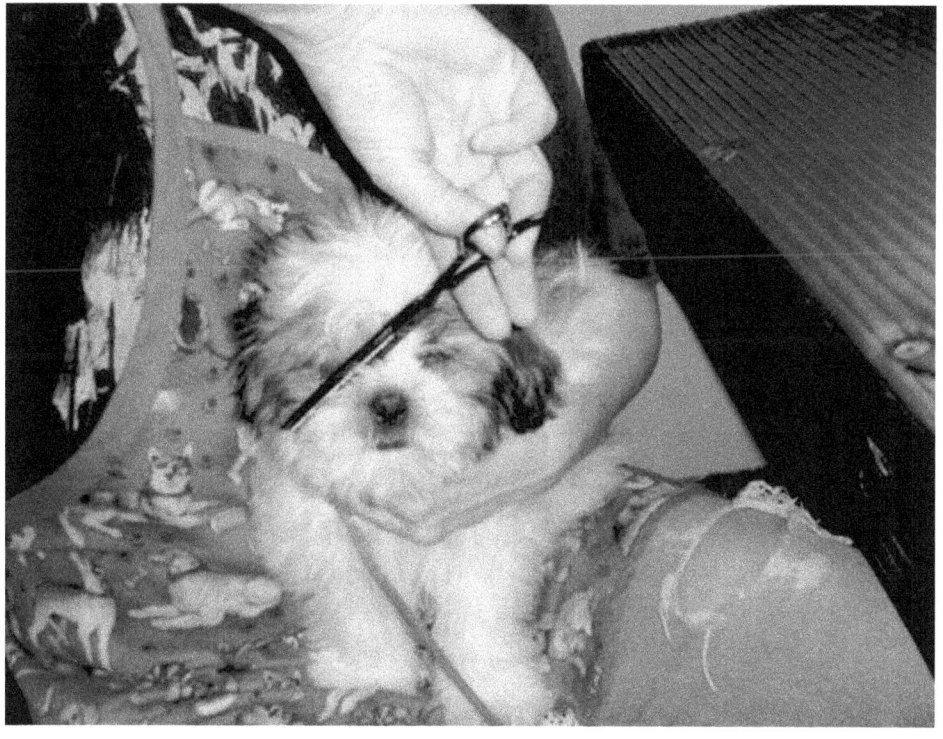

Or you can move the scissors and approach the eye with the end pointing up.

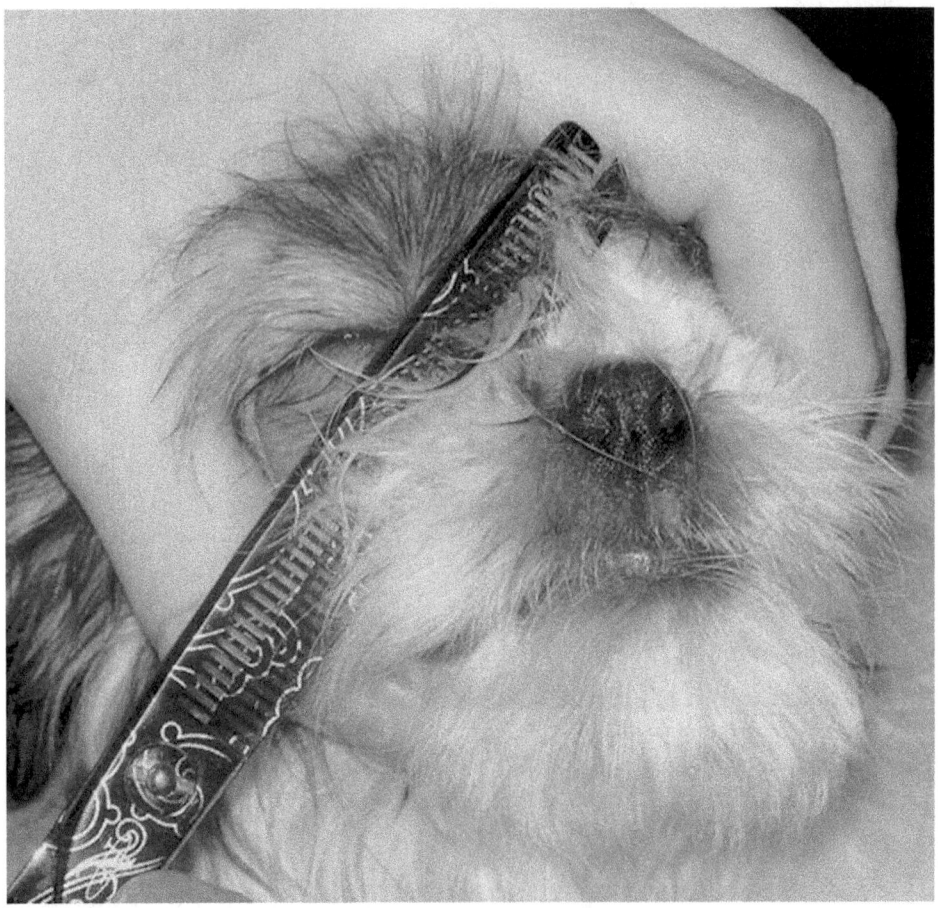

The choice is yours. It will depend on what the puppy is more comfortable with as well. If you decide to move the scissors so the end is pointing up, I suggest moving the puppy onto your lap. It's easier for you to hold the puppy's head and scissor at a comfortable angle.

The thinning shears emit a sound that for some reason is hypnotic to some dogs. I've had dogs fall asleep while I'm scissoring their head with thinning shears.

What to expect
Expect the puppy to move his head around to see what you are doing and what is making the noise. Murmur calmly to him and cup his face in your hand to steady his head. Don't be surprised if he falls asleep.

Final finish
Comb out the ears and shape with scissors. The majority of puppies will be a

limp rag in your arms by now, only wanting to sleep. Hold the puppy standing on his back legs with one hand to scissor stray hairs on the undercarriage. Holding the penis between your first two fingers, move your fingers forward, so the head of the penis is behind your fingers. Scissor the hair in front of your fingers. Your fingers act as a block, preventing a cut penis. Finish the puppy with his collar and bows or bandana, whichever you use in your shop.

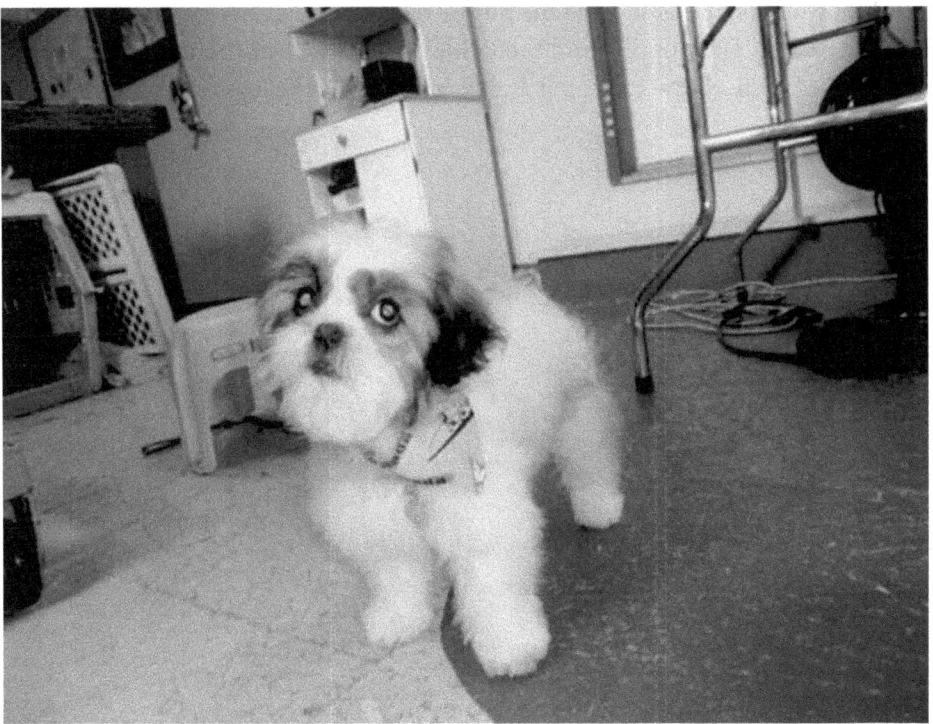

Give the puppy a play on the floor and a little treat. Call owners.

This is the groom for the first week, it sounds easier than it is. However, most puppies accept what you do to them as long as you do it in a calm manner. There is no need to pin the puppy or get mad. The face is by far the hardest part at this stage and how you approach it can dictate how the puppy will behave for each subsequent groom.

Troubleshooting the finish
Legs
Dogs are away-pressure animals. This means that if there is an uncomfortable pressure, they will move away from it. If they don't like you pulling on their legs, they will pull back to get away from the pressure. If a puppy pulls his leg back, instead of getting into a tugging match, push the leg back a couple of times and the puppy will relax. As soon as the puppy relaxes, praise. Always make sure you tell him to *Stop*. For puppies and even older dogs, I will sit them in my lap, hold the leg out by the elbow to keep it stable, and scissor the legs.

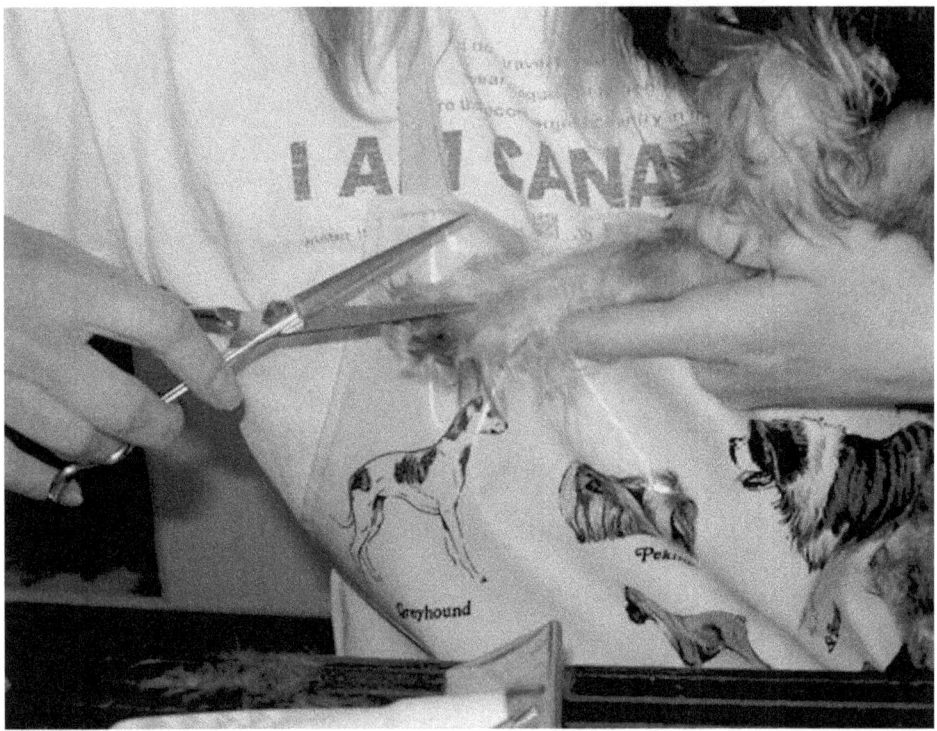

Face
Some puppies, no matter how tired they are, will fight you with their face. It always amazes me how a 12 week old puppy can be a menace when you try anything with its face. It is extremely important that these puppies learn at this age to accept having their face worked with and scissored.

If you have tried absolutely everything to scissor the puppy's face, here are some tricks I've used.

Rub the back of a spoon with some peanut butter (if there are peanut allergies in the house, substitute cheese spread for peanut butter). You can also rub a wiener or anything meaty that will leave a film on the spoon. Hold the end of the spoon in your mouth (I use a plastic spoon), so the back of the spoon is close enough so the puppy can lick it while you trim around the eyes.

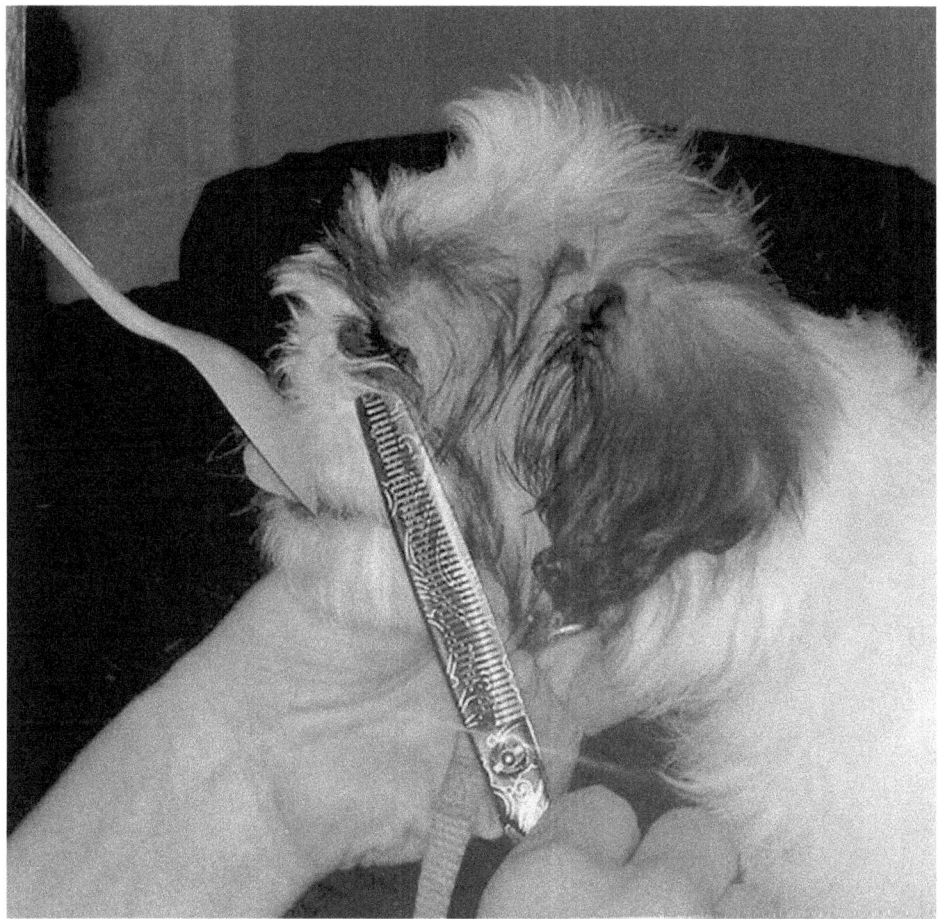

Peanut butter can be messy, especially if the dog is clean, so you want to put just a scant layer on the bowl of the spoon to prevent it from caking the fur around the mouth. I generally don't use any type of spread like peanut butter or cheese spread after the bath. Rubbing a wiener or hard cheese on the spoon has the same distraction and is less messy.

Turn the puppy into a sausage roll. Wrap the puppy in a towel so the legs are all tucked in, leaving just the head sticking out.

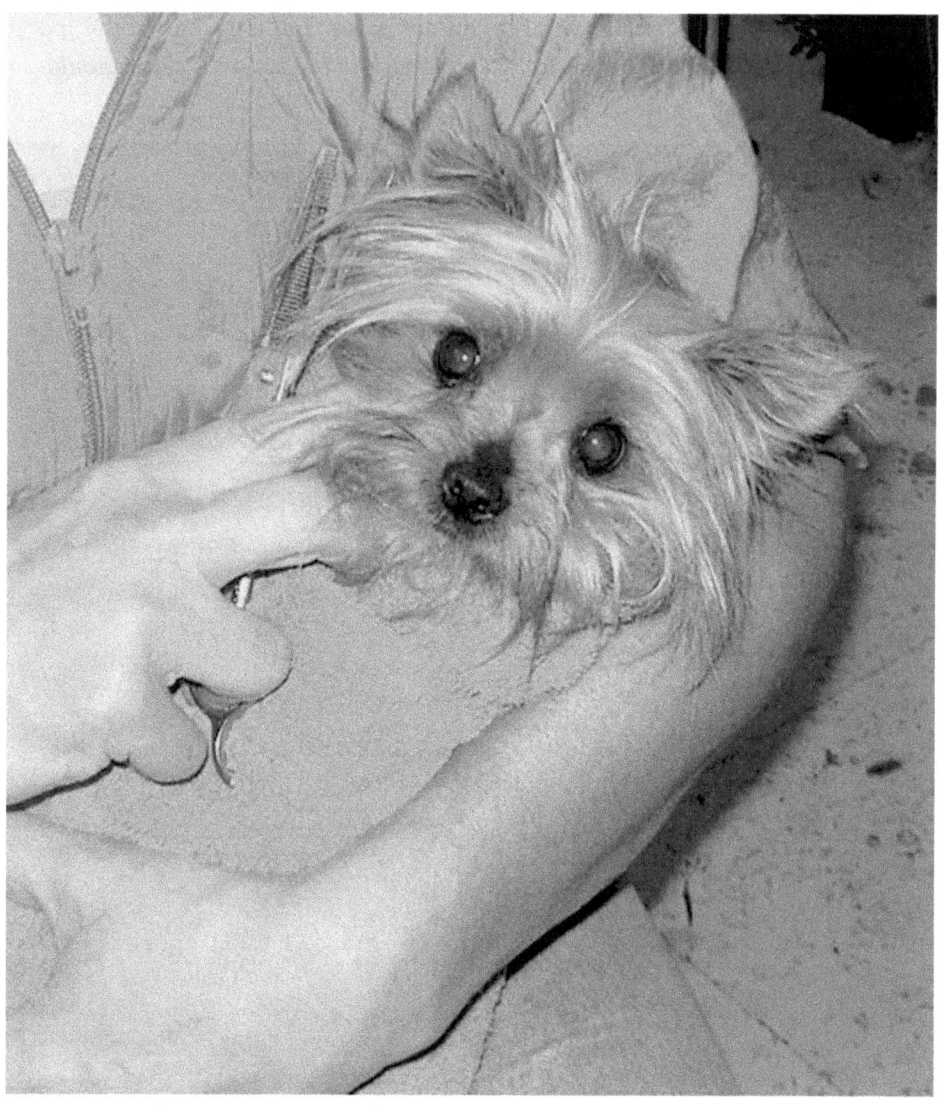

Make sure it is snug enough so the legs can't escape, but loose enough around the throat so the puppy isn't being choked. Cradle the puppy in one arm with the head tucked in the crook of your elbow and scissor with the other.

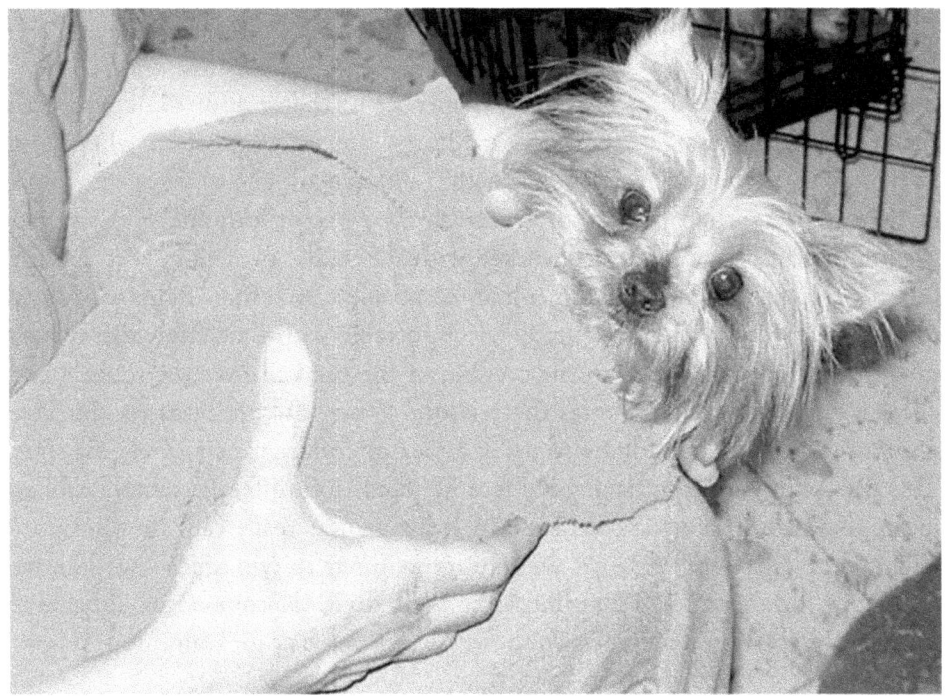

If this is uncomfortable for you, take your little sausage puppy and lay him on your lap so he is snuggled between your thighs.

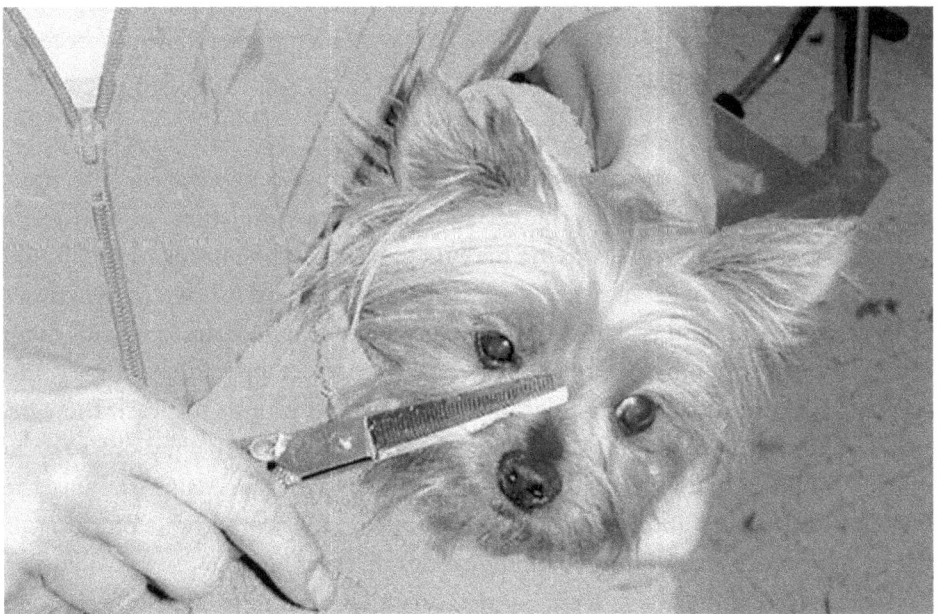

Support his head to keep it still and scissor the eyes.

I find that simply saying *shhhhhhhh* relaxes the puppy.

Homework for owners
Face
Some puppies need extra work. Every owner wants their puppy to do well with the grooming process. Many have heard horror stories of grooming shops and some have experienced bad grooms with a different dog. Knowing this, most owners are more than willing to work with their puppy at home. Explain that the puppy hates having his face worked with. Show the owners how to rub the puppy's eyes with your index finger and to rub and touch the whole face two to four times a week. When the puppy is comfortable with that, show the owners how to rub a popsicle stick in the crevices of the eye and over the muzzle and cheeks. A popsicle stick mimics the scissors. When the puppy is comfortable with a popsicle stick, graduate to using a pair of children's scissors taped shut. This gets puppy used to having his face handled, and different articles rubbed in the corner of his eyes and on his face. If the owners really can't do this or are having problems doing this, get them to come in one to two times a week, leave the puppy for about 15 to 20 minutes and you do it. Of course I would charge for it, my suggestion would be two to five dollars per visit for training.

Feet
Show the owners how to work with the feet by rubbing them, spreading the toes, rubbing each nail, and pretending to clip the nails. Make sure you emphasis pretending. Many dogs have issues with their nails from people cutting them too short and quicking the nail. It hurts. If it is done repeatedly, it may become impossible to cut the nails without a tranquilizer.

Ear plucking
Explain to the owner the importance of ear plucking to prevent ear infections that can be caused by hair in the ear canal that traps moisture. Inform them that their puppy doesn't like having his ears plucked and he needs to be worked with at home. Tell the owner that until the next groom and for two to four times each week they should reach into the ear, grab one or two hairs, and pull them out. Make sure they have a treat ready beside them to give to the puppy and to play as a reward. It doesn't matter if they take all month to pluck the ears. Emphasize that they should only do this once in a while, so they don't try to pluck a couple of hairs every time the puppy sits on their lap. Also make sure the owners rub the ears and massage the ears once in a while without plucking. If the owner plucks every time the puppy comes on their lap, the puppy will avoid the owner. Remember, dogs are away-pressure animals and will go away from an uncomfortable or hurtful pressure. Owners only have to pluck a couple of hairs at a time. For women, compare it to plucking eyebrows—it hurts the first time, but every time you do it, it hurts less and less. Men relate better to the example of

shaving after they have had a beard. The skin is sensitive, but toughens up after a few shaves. If the owners won't do it or are very uncomfortable doing it, offer for them to come in once or twice a week and you can pluck a couple of hairs out at a time. Again, charge them.

Chapter 6 Second Visit

A puppy at 16 weeks is much more confident than a 12 week old puppy and will investigate with confidence. They have no problem moving, growling, or snapping if you are doing something they don't like, which is pretty much everything. They are in the beginning stages of puberty.

If a groomer handles this stage aggressively or roughly, it will cause problems in subsequent grooms.

This visit is where I find most of the behaviour problems start. They are in their teenage stage, rebellious and wild. This visit is the hardest and most frustrating. Don't worry—this is normal. This is why we don't shave them between 12 to 16 weeks, unless there is no choice. They will fight you tooth and nail and it won't be a positive experience for either you or the dog if you get upset or mad. Forcing a puppy at this stage and imposing your will on him will cause him to fight back. Owners of dogs that have grooming issues can pinpoint that the problems started after the second groom when the dog was between 12 to 16 weeks. If you find yourself getting frustrated, put the puppy off the table. Do not yell, pin, hit, or take your frustrations out on the puppy. Put the puppy away. This visit will take the longest out of the three puppy visits in this program, so tell the owners you may need the puppy all day. Don't give them a pick up time. It will all depend on how the puppy does.

You must get through this visit calmly and with patience.

Meet and greet
This time with meet and greet you can be more jovial with the puppy. He is secure in his home and remembers the first experience in your shop as a positive one. Place a shop collar and leash on him and let him wander around the shop while you talk to the owners about this visit, explaining to them that this is the hardest visit he will experience because he is going through puberty and will need extra time. You may notice the attitude of the owner has also changed from being overprotective to gleefully telling you to take all the time you need as they hurry out the door. Let the puppy sniff around for a few minutes. Call the puppy, he should run to you. Scared or cautious puppies may freeze and need some coaxing to come to you. Place the puppy in a cage and either get the table ready, finish what you were doing before the puppy came in, or get ready to intake other dogs for the day. By putting the puppy in a cage for a bit, he is learning that in the grooming shop, sometimes he has to wait his turn. If the owners have been

crate training him, he should settle very quickly. If he starts whining or crying, simply cover cage or door of the cage to darken it to help him settle. Tough guys, royalty, and wild ones may tend to whine, bark or claw the cage door. Two methods I recommend to stop this is to spray him with a jet of water from a water gun or squirt bottle or have a can with a few pennies or marbles in it with the top taped shut and throw the can to land on the floor in front or beside the cage. This makes a loud sound and he will be shocked into silence. Repetition of both methods will be necessary until he learns that he won't get let out until he is calm and quiet. When puppies or dogs whine, bark or scratch to get out of the cage, it raises their anxiety which will also raise the anxiety of the other dogs in the shop. Dogs in a state of high anxiety are more difficult to groom. When he has settled down, let him out of the cage and put him on the table.

I refrain from over-praising puppies or dogs when they stop barking in the kennel. A soft *Good Dog* is sufficient. If you are jubilant in your praise for stopping barking, they will get excited and start barking again.

Hydraulic table

If you use a hydraulic table, make sure it is lowered for the large breed puppies. While sitting on the table hold the leash and coax the puppy to climb on the table beside you by patting the table and saying the word *Table*.

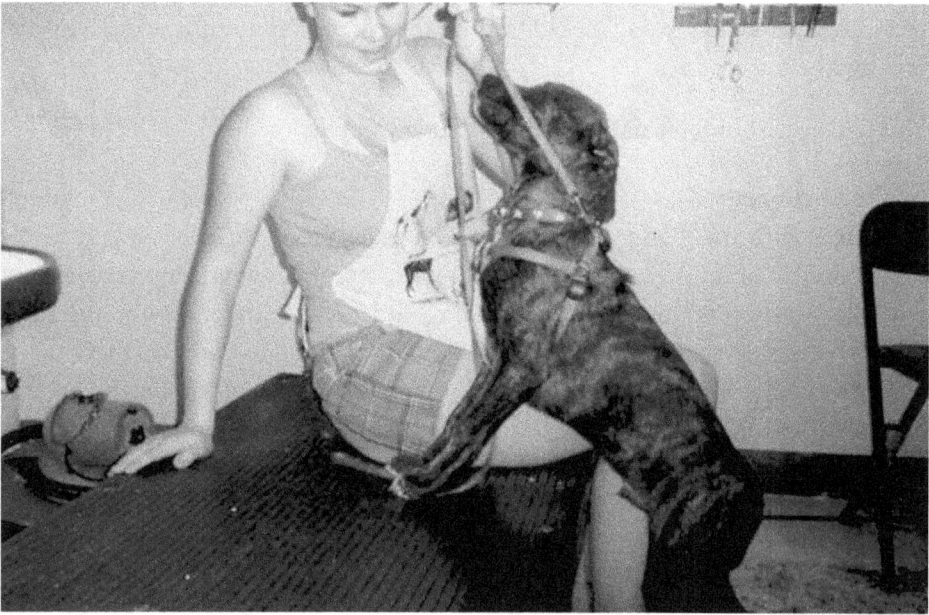

Some puppies will jump on the table immediately. Praise them. Other puppies may be wary of the table. Praise the puppy as soon as the he approaches the table.

The hesitant puppy will approach the table, then back away, then approach closer and back away, then approach with one paw on the table and back away. If the puppy won't put his paw on the table on his own, simply pick up the front end of the puppy and place both paws on the table and praise him. He may jump back right away—keep repeating it with you placing his front feet on the table. You will notice that each time there will be less resistance from the puppy and he will hold his front feet on the table for longer periods each time. When the puppy is leaving his front feet on the table or putting them on by himself, simply give him a lift from the back end to get the rest of his body on the table. Praise the puppy each time he progresses to get on the table. When the puppy is confident that it is safe, he will jump on the table when you say *Table*.

Keep the puppy on the table for at least 20 seconds and then repeat the command *Wait*, stand up and tell him *Off*, and then coax him off the table. Praise him when he jumps down. Pat the table, say *Table*, and praise him when he gets on. For a cautious puppy or shy puppy, you may have to sit on the table again to coax him on,

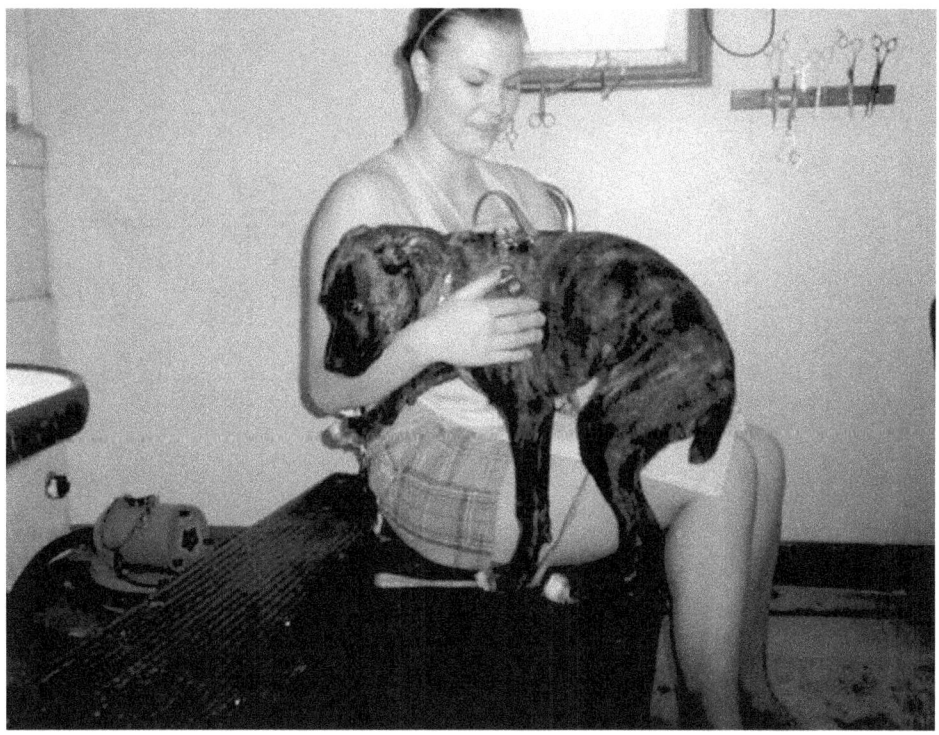

otherwise remain bent over the lowered table, patting the top, and telling the puppy *Table*. After 20 seconds, straighten up and tell the puppy *Off* and coax him off the table. Repeat this until the puppy is jumping onto the table and off the table when you tell it to. If the puppy jumps off without you saying *Off*, don't praise him, just get him back on the table, shorten the leash in your hand tell him *Wait* and hold him on the table for 20 seconds. Tell him *Off*, release your hold, and let him jump off.

He is learning to stay on the table until you give him the command *Off*.

Once the puppy is getting on and off the table easily, get him on the table, tell him to *Wait*, hold his collar, and raise the table six inches. Repeat *Wait* and hold him for 20 seconds. Lower the table, count to five, and tell him *Off*, releasing the collar allowing him to get off the table. Praise him and give him a play. Repeat the exercise, raising the table more each time until the table is raised to its highest point. The puppy may get nervous at a certain height. Talk to the puppy in a soothing voice while holding him in a wait command at this height. Pet him on the muzzle, head, and around the ears to relax him.

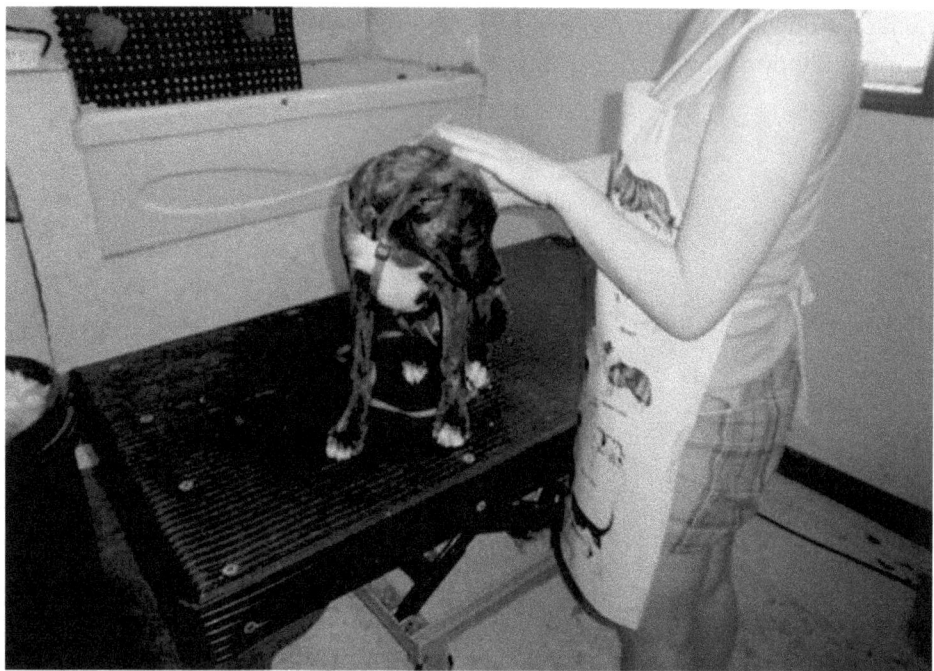

Repeat the height until the puppy is comfortable with being at that particular height before increasing the height of the table. Never let a puppy jump from the table until it is completely lowered. With very exuberant puppies you need to hang on to the collar to slow them down from leaping off the table when you give the command *Off*. They are still growing and can hurt themselves if they leap off too fast.

Steps/ramp

Follow the procedure for the hydraulic table, but instead of using *Table* and *Off*, simply use either *Step* or *Ramp*. When the puppy gets to the top of the steps or ramp, simply pat the tub, say *Tub*, and lead the puppy into the tub. You may have to help him down into the tub by physically lifting his front end and putting him into the tub. Hold onto the collar, tell him to *Wait*, keep him in the tub for 20 seconds, and then lead him to the steps or ramp, tell him *Steps* or *Ramp*, and lead him down to the floor. Repeat this exercise until the puppy is confidently walking up, into the tub, and out again.

Pre-bath groom

Equipment needed:

> Thinning Shears
> Straight edge shears (rounded or blunted end)
> Pin or slicker brush which ever is appropriate for the coat
> Comb
> Deshedding comb, if grooming a short hair dog
> Nail clippers
> Nail grinder (if available)
> Clippers

Bring the puppy onto the table, and put the noose on. Keep the arm for the noose lowered, so the puppy still has room to move.

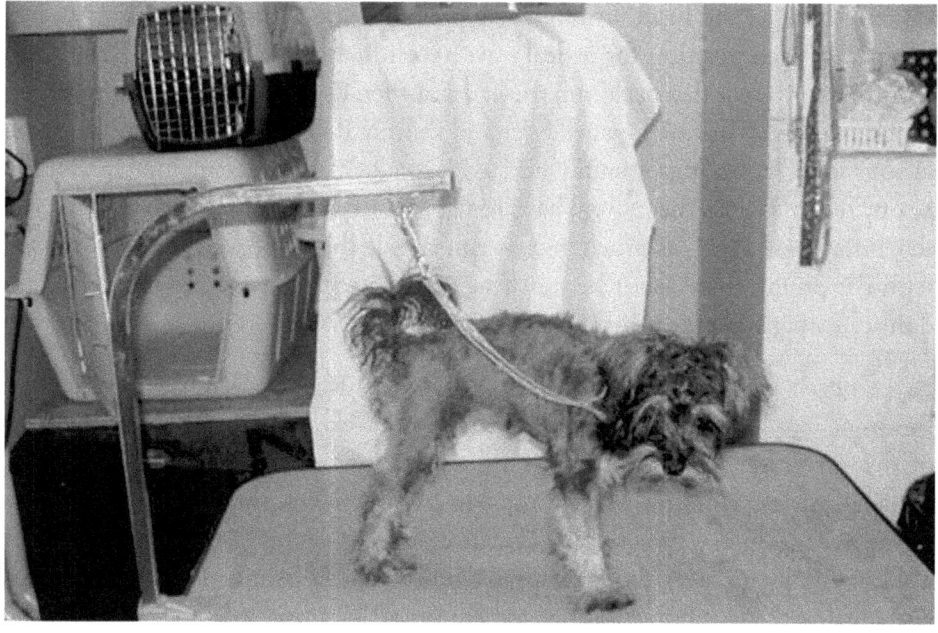

If you have the puppy noosed high during this stage, you will have a battle on your hands, as the puppy will fight the noose and you. Keeping a lot of slack in the noose holds the puppy, but allows him enough movement without him feeling that he's in a life threatening position. Leave a collar on the puppy so you can control the head if needed. The noose is not meant to be used as a control tool, merely a tool to hold a dog in position. If you leave a shop collar on the puppy, you can slip a finger under the collar to steady the head. Nooses can become loose at the worst possible moment and increase the chance of injury to the puppy or dog if the groomer relies on it for anything other than a tether to hold the dog on the table.

Touch and feel

Stroke the puppy starting at the muzzle and work your way all over the body as in the first visit. Repeat the *Stop* exercise as in the first visit. This visit though, instead of holding the puppy in a *Stop* position, you will put both hands on either side, say *Stop* in a firm, quiet voice, remove your hands, give the command *Stay*, count to three, and praise him. Each time you perform the *Stop* exercise, let the puppy stay motionless for longer periods on time, repeating the *Stay* command. Practice the stand exercise as in the first visit, but accompany the *Stand* command with the *Stay* command.

Positions

Practice holding the head in different positions as you did in the first visit, but again hold each position for at least five seconds. Look into the eyes, ears, and mouth. Flip the ear flap back, rub the ear, and then dust the hair with ear powder. Pluck a few hairs out with your finger and thumb. If you use an ear plucking tool in your shop, let the puppy sniff it and use it to pluck out the remaining hair. If the puppy rebels against the tool, go back to using your finger and thumb to pluck the remaining hair. Pluck as much hair as you can. If the owners have been working with the puppy, there won't be much hair in the ear. Rub the ear when you are done plucking and repeat for the other ear.

Extend each leg as in the first visit, however this time you are going to extend the front legs a bit further and hold them in an extended position for a count of five seconds. Gradually increase the length of time you keep the legs in a certain position. Hold the legs in positions by the elbows, the knees, and the toes. Remember to praise the puppy and if the puppy starts to struggle while you're holding his legs, repeat *Stop* and praise him when he stops moving. Extending and moving the legs into positions for grooming are unnatural positions and the puppy will offer resistance. Keep in mind, he is also growing and the positions may also be uncomfortable, refrain from over-extending the legs, especially if you are extending the legs out to the side. Avoid a tug of war to keep the leg in position; it is very easy at this age to pull a muscle or strain a joint.

Use the appropriate brush for the coat of the dog and do a pre-bath brush, starting with the front left leg and working your way around the dog. When you get to the anus, brush any feces out of the fur if you are able to. For feces that is clumped, wait until you are using scissors to cut it out. Remember, let the puppy sniff the brush first so he knows what to expect. If you are grooming a short-haired puppy, introduce a deshedding tool and gently brush him with it.

With the thinning shears and scissors, repeat the exercise as in the first visit, rubbing the scissors on the body starting with the front left leg. After you have rubbed the shears and scissors on the puppy, extend the front left leg, tell the puppy to *Stop*, then *Stand*, and then rub the shears along the leg in the same series of motions you would do to shape the leg. Place the leg back on the table and praise the puppy. Pick up the leg again, extend it, and this time go through the motions of shaping the leg with the shears, but hold the shears between half an inch to an inch away from the fur on the leg. Open and close the shears as if you were shaping the leg. When the puppy squirms, firmly tell him to *Stop*, wait for him to stop, and then praise him and carry on. Practice this exercise for the whole dog.

When you come to the butt, practice fake cutting first, then scissor any feces stuck to the fur. If there is feces stuck very close to the skin, wait until the bath to work it out.

Rub the shears over the head, starting at the back of the head and working your way towards the stop of the dog. Rub the scissors on the face as in the first visit, starting at the base of the ear working towards the muzzle. Rub the shears in each crevasse of the eyes with the shears closed. This will give you a good idea if the owners have been working with the puppy at home if you had recommended it. Let the puppy off the table for a play and a treat.

You will be surprised by how much this puppy remembers. By repeating the first week's lessons on the table, you are re-establishing what the puppy learned the first week. The puppy begins to understand that this is work and that he must behave in a certain manner in the grooming shop. He may also rebel against it. But just keep re-establishing the training. Because he is older, you can go longer on the table without always having to give him a play. Be aware of the puppy's emotional state; if he starts getting antsy or stressed, put him off the table for a play.

Nail grinder

When you are ready to do the nails, and if you have a grinder, now is the time to introduce the puppy to a nail grinder. Show the puppy the grinder and let him sniff it and lick it while it is off. Hold it away and turn it on. Let the puppy get used to the noise, but don't let him sniff it while it is on. Whiskers and tongues can easily get caught. Hold the puppy's foot and clip the nails. Continue holding the foot and then turn on the grinder and hold it in front of each toe, pretending to grind each nail, but not actually grinding them.

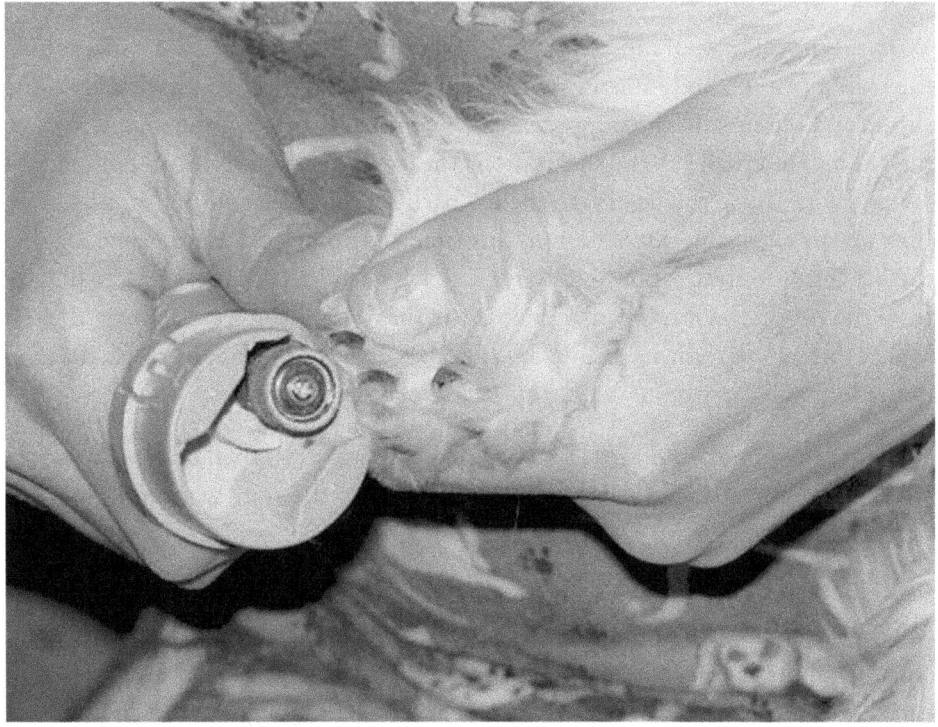

You are giving the puppy a sound to associate with his nails in a safe manner. Do this with each foot.

Clippers

Before the bath, introduce the clippers. He has already sniffed them and heard them, but this time you are going to run them over his body while they are turned on. There are two ways to do this safely. You can use a blade or blade with a comb clip, but always have a blade on the clippers. Running the clippers over the body without a blade increases the chances of catching the fur in the moving parts of the clippers. Turn on the clippers and let puppy sniff them, watch that he doesn't lick them and cut his tongue.

With the clippers on, move the clippers as if you are grooming the puppy, but hold the clippers about three inches away from the body. The puppy will spin around to watch the clippers and may want to sniff them again.

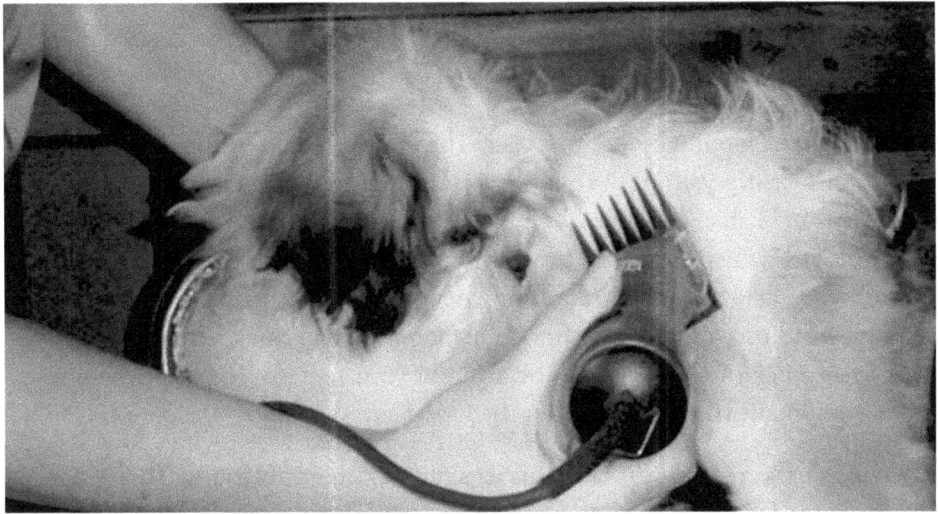

Let him sniff them again to satisfy his curiosity that the clippers are not hurting him. This exercise teaches the puppy that the clippers can move around his body. When the puppy gets bored of the clippers moving around his body, hold the clippers backwards over the back so the cutting part of the blade is pointing towards the front of the dog. You're not cutting hair right now; you are exposing the puppy to the sensation of having the clippers on his body while they are running. Starting in the middle of the back, run the clippers towards the tail. You are just running them over the puppy without actually clipping any fur. Continue to do this on the back until puppy gets comfortable with the feeling and stops jumping around. When he is accepting the clippers on his back, move the clippers up to the base of the neck and move them down the back to the base of the tail. When the puppy is comfortable with that, move them up to the base of the skull and run them down the neck to the base of the tail. Then starting at the spine, run them down the shoulder and the outside of front leg, then sides, then back legs running the clippers down the hip to the foot, the butt, the tail and then the other side. Run them from the chin down the chest, then the inside, back, and front of each leg. Starting at the base of the skull, move the clippers about half of inch onto the head and run them to the neck. Increase the distance on the head each pass. Flip the ear back, go onto the cheek about half inch from the ear, and run them back past the ear down the side of the neck, gradually increasing the distance on the cheek until you are running the clippers from the muzzle all the way back. Run them over the ear flap and on the inside of the ears. Stand puppy up on hind legs and run them on the undercarriage, abdomen, and inside flank area. Make sure you run the clippers on the pads of each foot.

When you move the clippers over the puppy without cutting the fur, the puppy becomes accustomed to the vibration of the clippers in a safe, controlled manner.

What to expect

Expect to use a lot of patience this visit. The puppy will move, swing around, and dance his feet everywhere. Whenever you touch him, he will move and it will seem he is ticklish everywhere. When you turn on a piece of equipment, he will follow it and will spin around as you move it around his body. The puppy will not just taste brushes and scissors, but chew and bite at them. He will swing and fling his head to avoid the scissors on his face. He will duck his head when you look in or pluck the ears. He will be nippy at your fingers. The puppy will try to avoid equipment you introduced in the first visit.

He will fight you when you move his legs into different positions. This is normal for the second visit. Be calm and persistent.

Troubleshooting
Front legs
When you have the front leg extended forward and the puppy tries to pull his leg back, simply push his leg back in the direction he is trying to pull and extend it again. You may have to repeat this a few times. Each time you extend the leg, repeat *Stop*. If the puppy starts to panic or bite at you, extend the leg by holding the elbow rather than the foot and hold it in an extended position.

Back legs
The puppy may spin around to see what you are doing to his back legs. Let him watch, he wants to assure himself that you aren't hurting him.

When you extend the back leg to the rear of the puppy and the puppy starts to pull back on it, ease up on the extension so the leg isn't extended quite so far back. You may be extending it beyond the comfort zone of the puppy. When you are lifting the leg up and off to the side and the puppy sits, again, don't lift it so high. By sitting, the puppy is telling you that you are lifting too high and it is uncomfortable. If the puppy attacks you, it means that it hurts.

Face
If you get a puppy that is completely unmanageable with his face while on the table, put the puppy in your lap either sitting with his back against your stomach or lying on your lap.

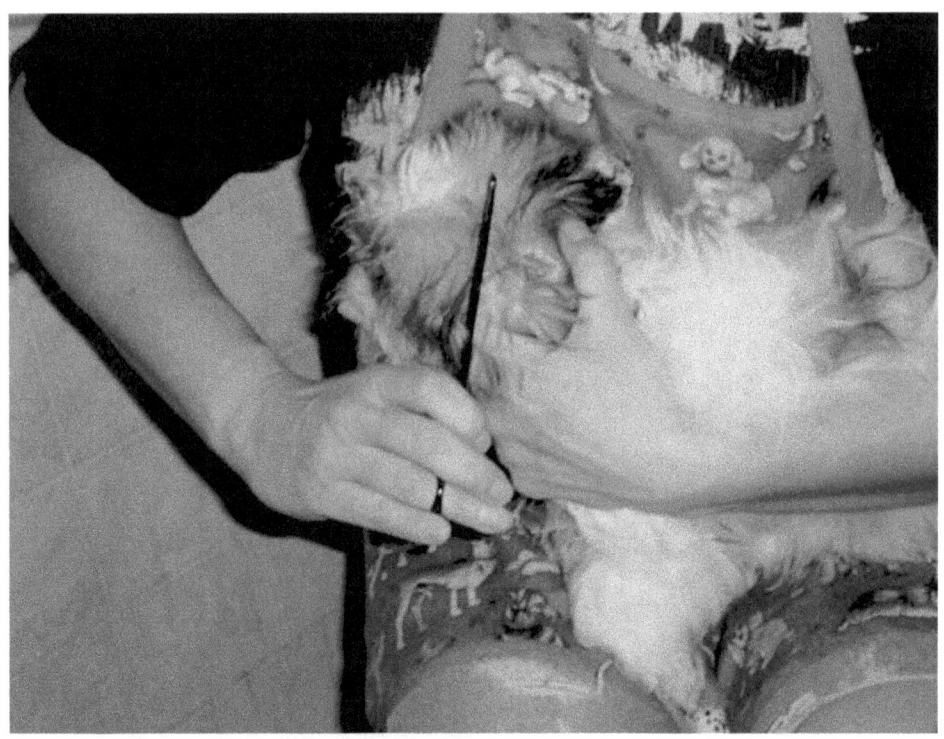

Hold his head with your hand clasped around the side of his head and his muzzle between your first two fingers with your index finger on top of the muzzle and your middle finger under the muzzle.

In this position, rub the scissors in the eye crevasses. Start the scissors at the outside corner of the eye and slide them to the inside corner of the eye. Don't forget to rub in between the eyes.

Another head hold I use on puppies is to hold the head from above, wrapping your fingers in a claw-like fashion around the head. You can also sausage roll the puppy as in the first visit.

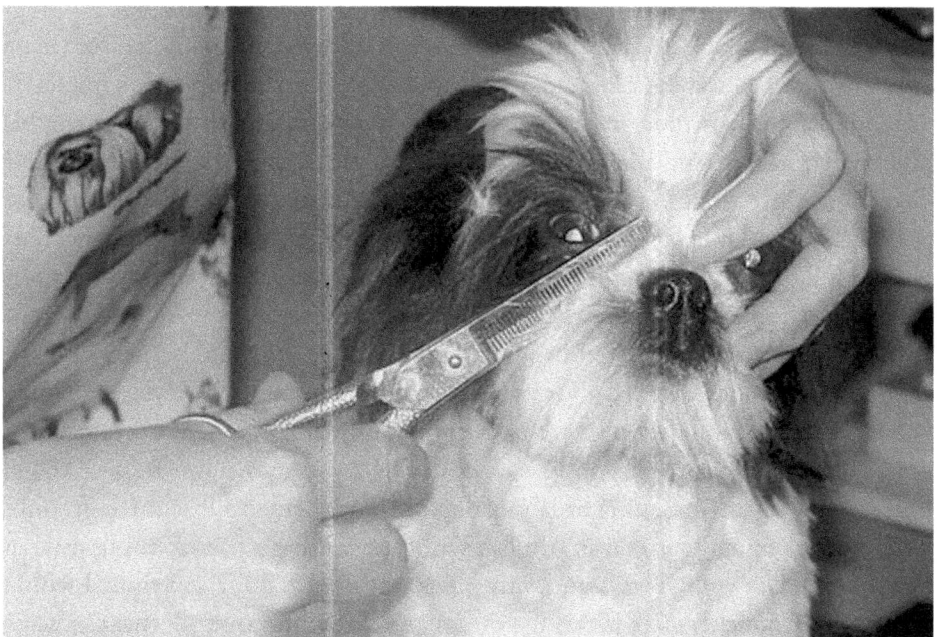

Brush
If the puppy keeps spinning every time you put the brush on him, hold his head by the collar with his face looking at yours. Repeat *Stop* as much as you want, hold him in position by the collar, and brush him all over. Use small strokes to accustom him to the feel of being brushed. Puppies are very sensitive to everything during this age.

Nails
Follow the troubleshooting as in the first visit. If the strategies don't work, cut the nails while puppy is in the tub either during or after the bath. If that's too much of a rodeo, trim the nails while finishing the puppy. Don't trim all the nails at once. Trim each foot as you are finishing the leg and foot. Many puppies and dogs work better if you trim the nails on one foot, then finish the leg and foot, then move to the next foot, rather than trimming the nails on all four feet one after the other.

Ear plucking
Hold the puppy's face cradled in both hands, rub the ear canal with your thumb, and gently pinch a few hairs between your thumb and finger. You have to do this by feel. Gently ease the hair out of the ear rather that yanking it out. As with

nails, spread the time out between ears. Pluck one ear, move to a different part of the body, and then pluck the other ear. Or wait until after the bath and dry to sausage roll the puppy as in visit one. If you can pluck one ear, but not the other, put the puppy on an alternate ear plucking schedule. I have many dogs that will let me pluck one ear during a visit, but both ears is too much for them, so every visit I pluck the alternate ear. It works well. If the puppy is completely unmanageable with plucking the ears and the owners are also having trouble plucking at home, send the owners to the vet to pluck the ears. The puppy may have an ear infection. Veterinarians usually have more staff to hold a puppy for ear plucking and it is far easier to train a puppy for ear plucking if the ears aren't packed full of hair. When talking to the owners, stress that they try to continue plucking at home. Remember this is a partnership between you and the owners. If the owners aren't interested in working with you for a trouble spot with the puppy, tell them it's very hard for you to work the hair out whenever the puppy comes in for a groom. If you have to pin the puppy down or if it takes three of you to pluck the ears of a puppy during this age, you may never be able to get near the ears again, including brushing or trimming them in subsequent grooms. Try to get as much hair out as you can without creating a panicked puppy that attacks you. Use your fingers and only pluck one or two hairs at a time. I would never put ear pluckers in the ear of a puppy that is flailing around; that's a recipe for injury.

Bath

Bath the puppy as in the first visit. If feces is stuck on the fur or close to the skin, comb or pick it out during the second shampoo cycle. It is much softer and easier to work out in the bath after soaking in water and shampoo.

What to expect
Expect a rodeo. The puppy may try to attack the water from the hose

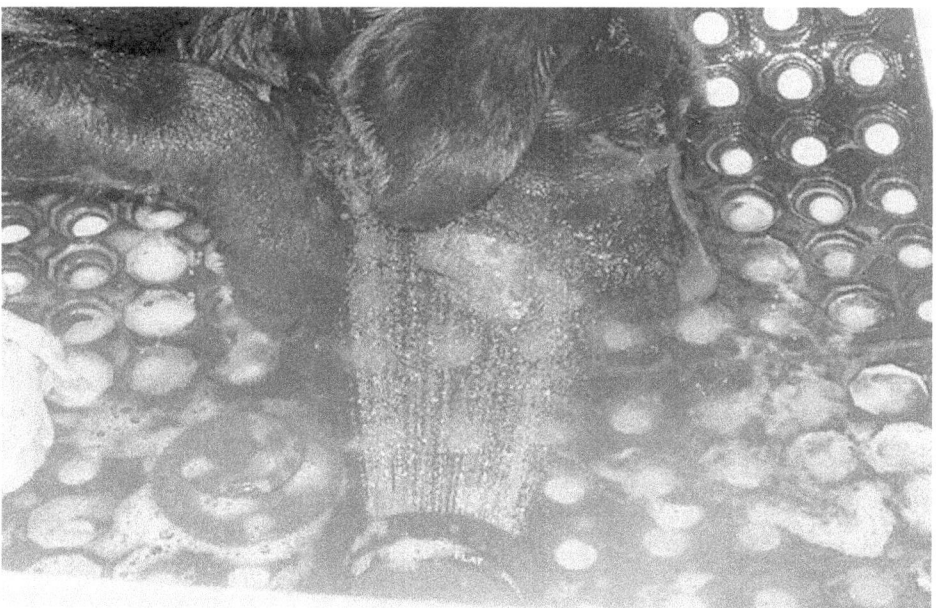

and try desperately to clamber out of the tub.

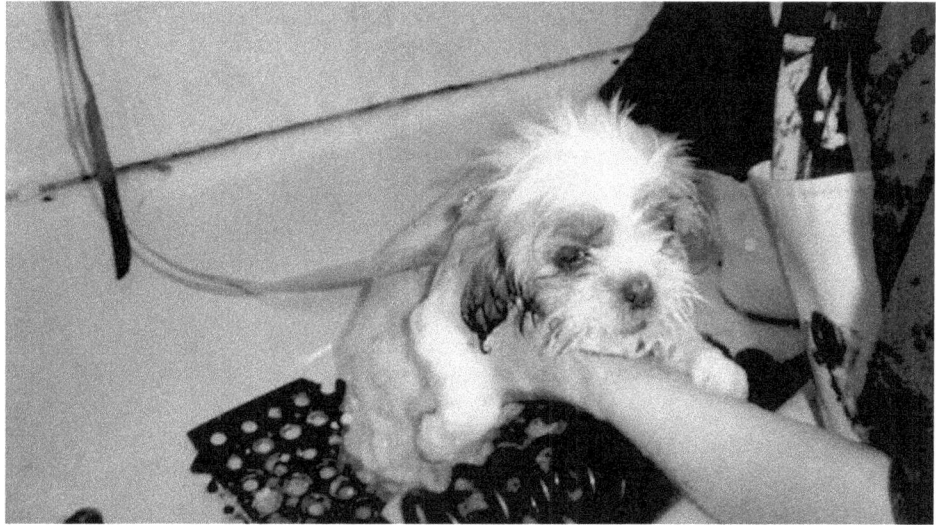

Expect to get wet this visit!

Troubleshooting the bath

Keep a collar or harness on the puppy during the bath, hold on to the collar or harness, and get through the bath as quickly as possible.

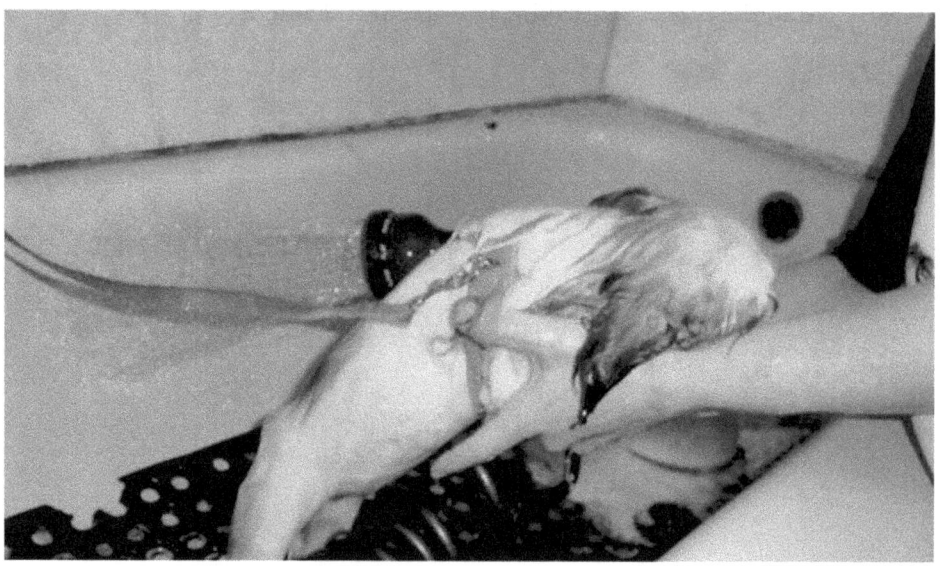

If the puppy panics when rinsing the head with the hose, flush the shampoo by pouring water over his head repeatedly until the water runs clear.

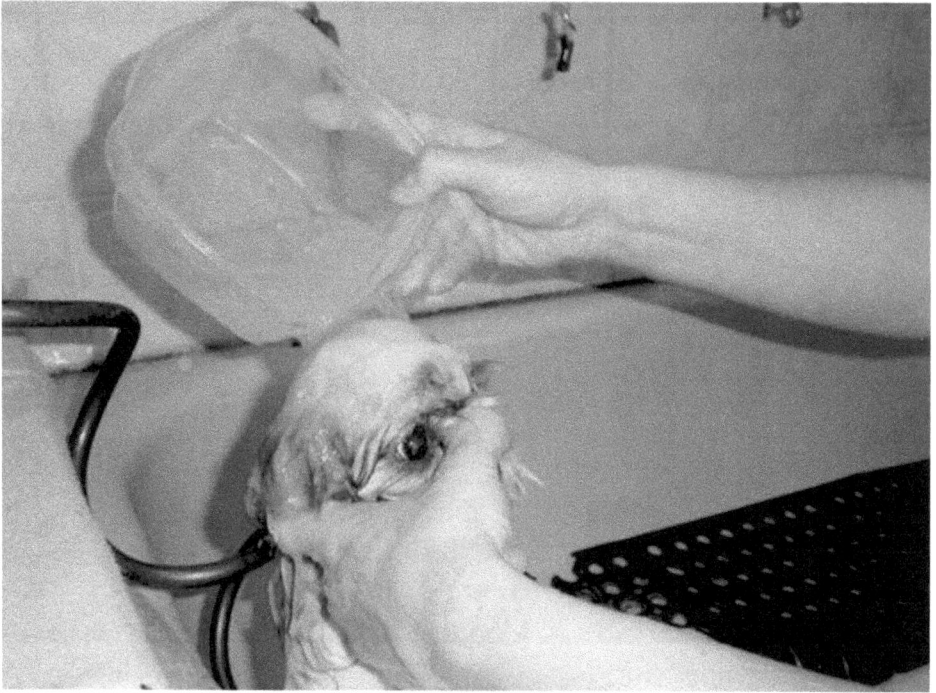

High voltage dryer

After the bath and towel dry, either keep the puppy in the tub or move the puppy to the drying area. Please don't tag the puppy up and start blowing your high velocity dryer at him randomly. This is a perfect way to scare him of not only a high velocity dryer, but also vacuums at home. Many dogs have a fear of vacuums that originated in the grooming shop as many high velocity dryers sound like vacuums.

Allow the puppy to be able to hold onto your arm or press against you. Turn on the high velocity dryer. The puppy will jump and may try to climb you to get away from the noise. Let him get used to the noise before you start drying him. He should have already been introduced to the noise in the first visit, so he should settle quickly. Keeping the nozzle close to the skin, start at the hips and lower back and direct the air towards the tail. The puppy may panic. Let him grip you or press against you and keep blowing it on his back and hips. Once the puppy realizes that he isn't being killed, maimed, or hurt, he will settle down or at least stop screaming. Working from the back to front, inch the flow of air up towards the head and chest. Dogs hate having air blown in their faces. Wait until the fourth or fifth visit before attempting to dry a dog's face with a high velocity dryer.

For sound and touch sensitive dogs, move the dryer around the puppy without actually blowing air on him.

If you don't have a high velocity dryer, as in the case of most pet owners, simply turn on a vacuum close to the puppy. This allows him to be introduced to the noise in a safe controlled manner.

After the high velocity dryer, cage or hand dry as you did in the first visit.

Finishing

When finishing the puppy for the second visit, run the clippers over his body, turned on, as you did before the bath, with the blade pointing backwards so no hair is being cut. Clip the pads with a #10 or #15 blade. Clip the hair flush with the pads.

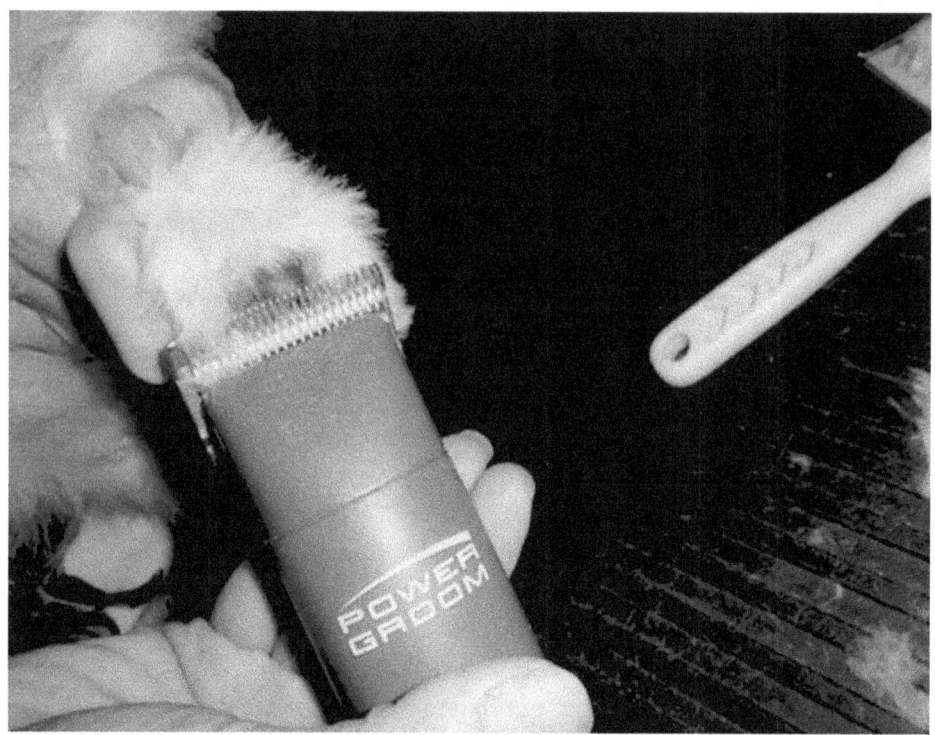

Only if the puppy is comfortable with clippers on his feet, can you clip the hair between the pads, otherwise leave it until next visit. Poodles are the exception. If the Poodle is comfortable with the clippers on and around his toes, clip the toes and feet, otherwise scissor the feet puffy and wait until next visit to do full Poodle feet. You may find that a Poodle puppy who didn't blink an eye when you clippered the toes in the first visit is fighting this visit. Remember, this is the puberty stage. If the Poodle puppy is fighting you, don't clipper the feet into Poodle feet this visit, you run a high risk of cutting the webbing between the toes, which may result in a Poodle that won't let you near his feet in the future.

Holding the puppy in your lap, touch the nail grinder to the tips of the nails. Again, if the puppy panics—stop. Use the clippers on the pads of feet (as explained above), anus area, and behind the ears. Scissor any stray hairs on the body and scissor the legs and feet. Use thinning shears on the face and around the eyes, as in the first visit. Trim the ears. Finish with bows or bandanas.

All puppies are taught the same thing in visits one and two—whether they are a Shih Tzu or a Doberman. Now why would I run clippers on a Doberman or a German Shepherd when the dog will never be shaved? Simple—you don't know if that dog will ever have to have a cut shaved on its leg or a spot shaved on its body. You may have to shave out tar or gum from between its pads when the puppy is a 90-pound German Shepherd. It will make everyone's life easier if the dog has been exposed to the sound and feel of the clippers when it is young. For many dogs, the first time they experience clippers is when they get neutered or spayed. When the dog is being anaesthetized for surgery, the last thing they hear before they are fully asleep is the clippers. When they wake up, very important body parts are missing. It's been my experience, that neutered male dogs (more so than females) are more nervous with clippers around their anus area if they weren't introduced to the sound and feel of the clippers prior to neutering.

What to expect
Expect the puppy to dance with his feet when you finish them. He will try to spin or sit when you clipper his butt. He may resist his face being scissored. Puppies at this age will not be tired after the bath and may be difficult to groom.

Troubleshooting the finish

Follow the troubleshooting instructions for the first week for different parts of the body. If the owners have been working at home with the puppy, it will be easier to work with the trouble areas or 'red zones'.

If the puppy has a red zone (a place where he flips out from the clippers), work with that spot by rubbing it with your hands and then scissor with thinning shears, move the clippers backwards over the spot (so blade won't cut the hair as explained in introducing the clippers), and try again with the blade in position to cut hair. If the puppy still panics, use the scissors. Red zones for a lot of puppies are the front legs, face, and butt.

Body/legs
Hold the puppy in your lap and run the clippers backwards over the body and legs. Many puppies will feel safer if they are sitting on your lap while learning about the clippers.

Feet

If the puppy is dancing with his feet while you are trying to scissor a rounded foot, simply pick up the front leg that you are not shaping and hold it.

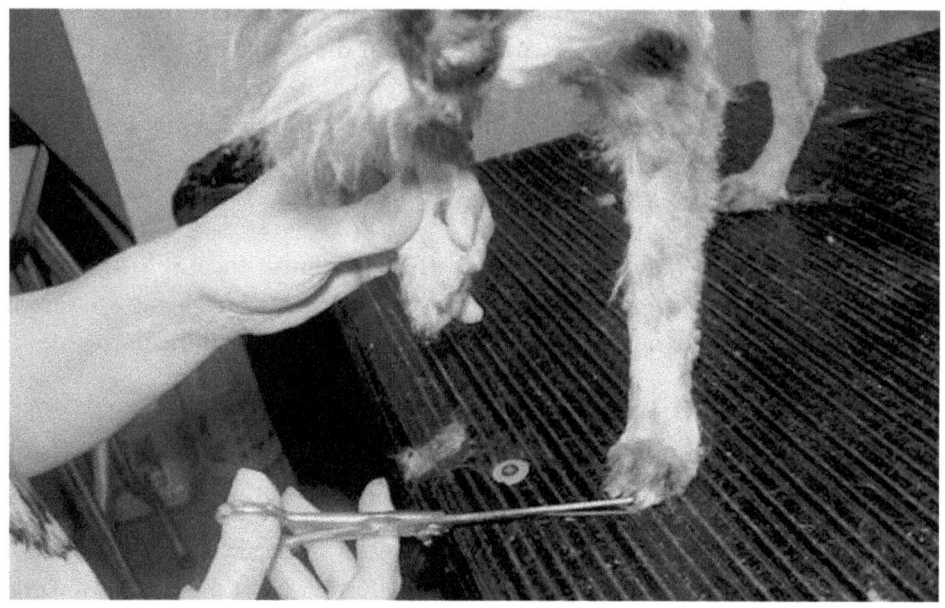

This will force the puppy to keep the foot you are shaping on the table.

Hold the puppy on your lap and scissor the feet while he's snuggled into you.

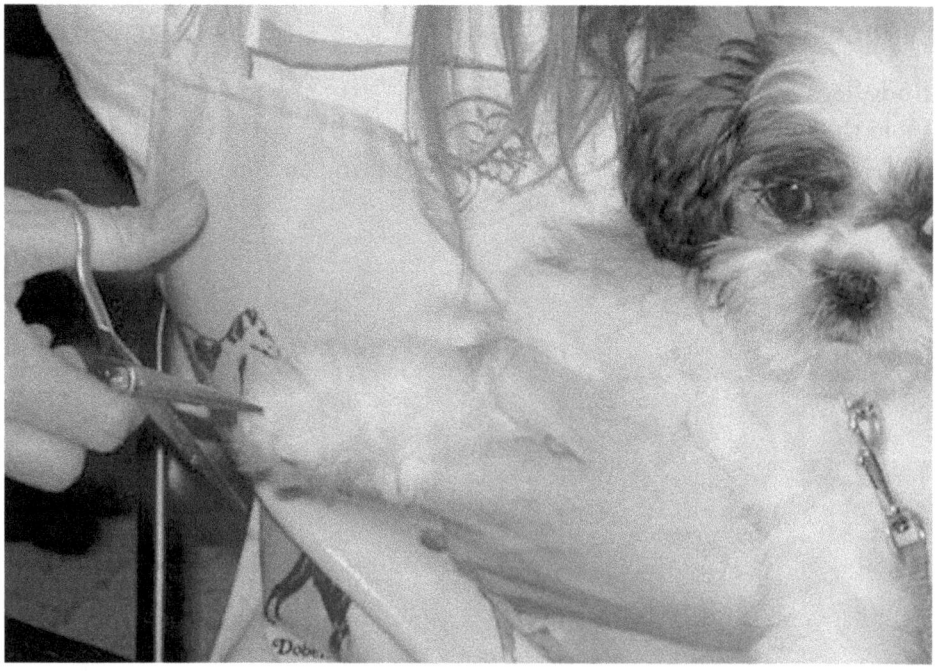

Face
Follow the troubleshooting strategies in the first visit.

Butt
Don't clip the hair close to the skin, as this will irritate the puppy. Clip the hair about half an inch long and use the clippers to shape a poop chute.

Nail grinder
If you are able to touch the grinder to at least two nails, you are doing well. The puppy can be sitting in your lap while teaching the nail grinder.

Homework For owners
Follow up on the homework for the owners in the first visit for feet, face, and ear plucking. If the owners have been doing the homework, you should notice a difference in the puppy. Tell them they are doing a great job with the puppy. Urge the owners that haven't been practicing the homework to please practice.

Chapter 7 The Third Visit

The last and final visit for the puppy program is here. Yippee! When the owner brings in the puppy, take some time to discuss different styles for the puppy. Repeat visit one and two for table work.

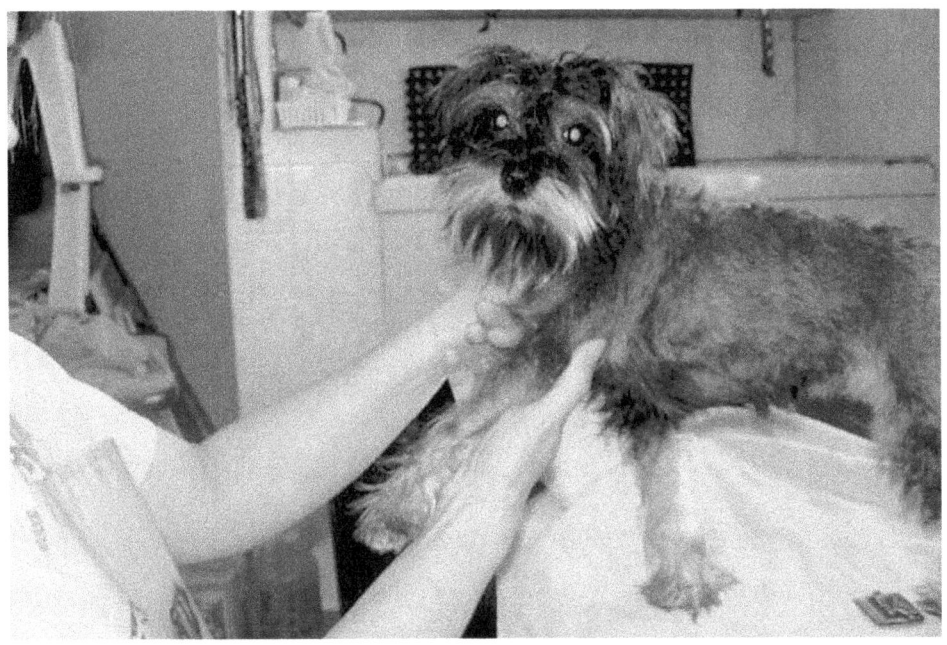

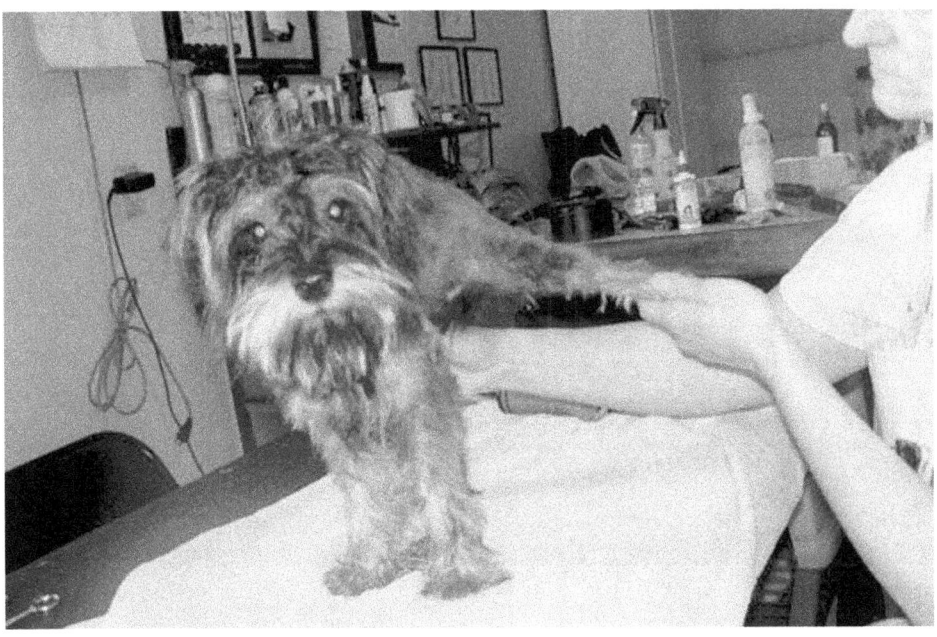

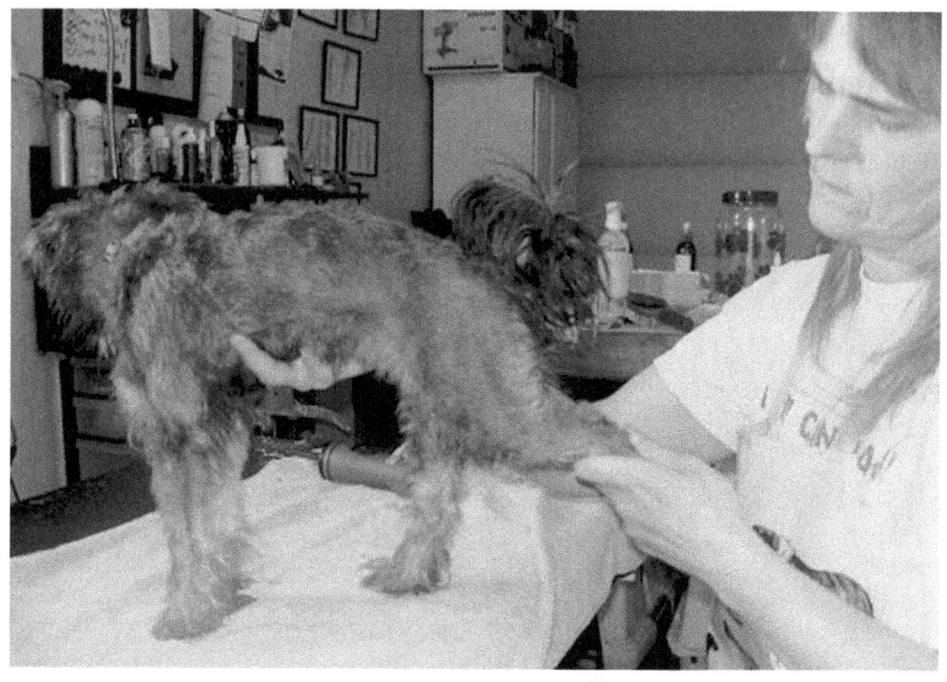

The noose (if you use one) can be raised to a comfortable height for the puppy.

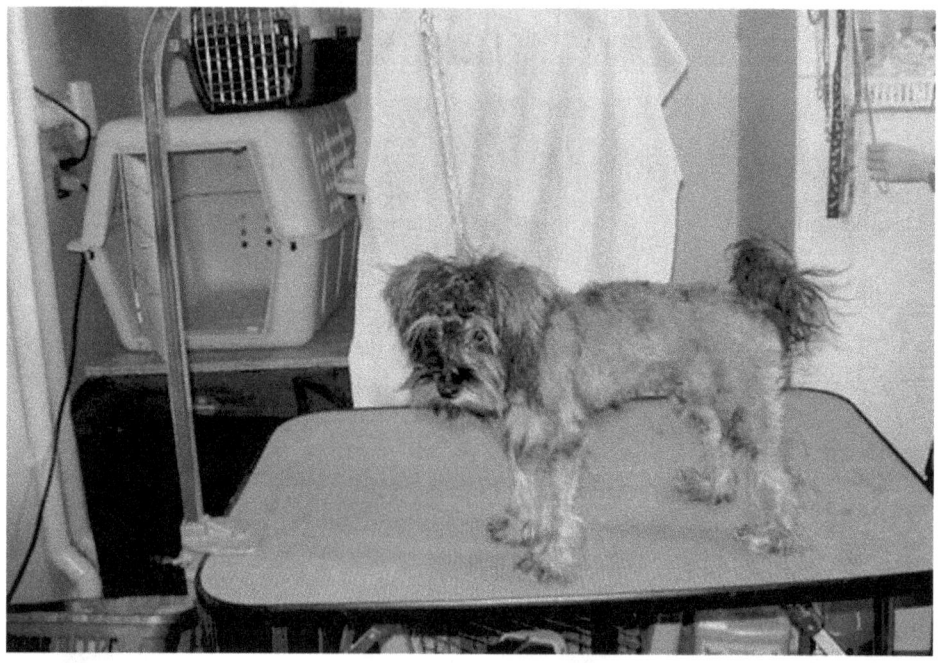

Keep it loose so the puppy isn't in a tight hanging position.

Ear plucking
This is the time to introduce ear pluckers. An ear plucking tool is a surgical forceps. To pluck the ears with a tool, grasp a few hairs and lock the handle. Twist the tool to wrap the hair around the end. When the hair is tightly wrapped, gently pull the tool straight out of the ear. The hair should come out easily. The trick is not to wrap too much hair. The less hair the easier it will be to pull out and it will be less painful on the puppy.

Nails
If your usual routine in grooming dogs is to do the nails before the bath, follow that routine for this visit and each visit afterwards. The nails are much thicker as the puppy is reaching adulthood in body and mind. Most puppies will readily accept having all their nails done by the grinder in this visit. For those puppies that won't accept the grinder, use nail clippers and give the nails a quick file with a nail file to smooth out any rough edges.

Pre-clip

You will be surprised with the maturity of the puppy and how different he is from the second visit. If you do a pre-clip before the bath to set the pattern, run the blade backwards a few times and then proceed to set the pattern. Go slow. Give the puppy time to get used to the sensation of hair coming off. Start at the lower back and hips, gradually moving to the front.

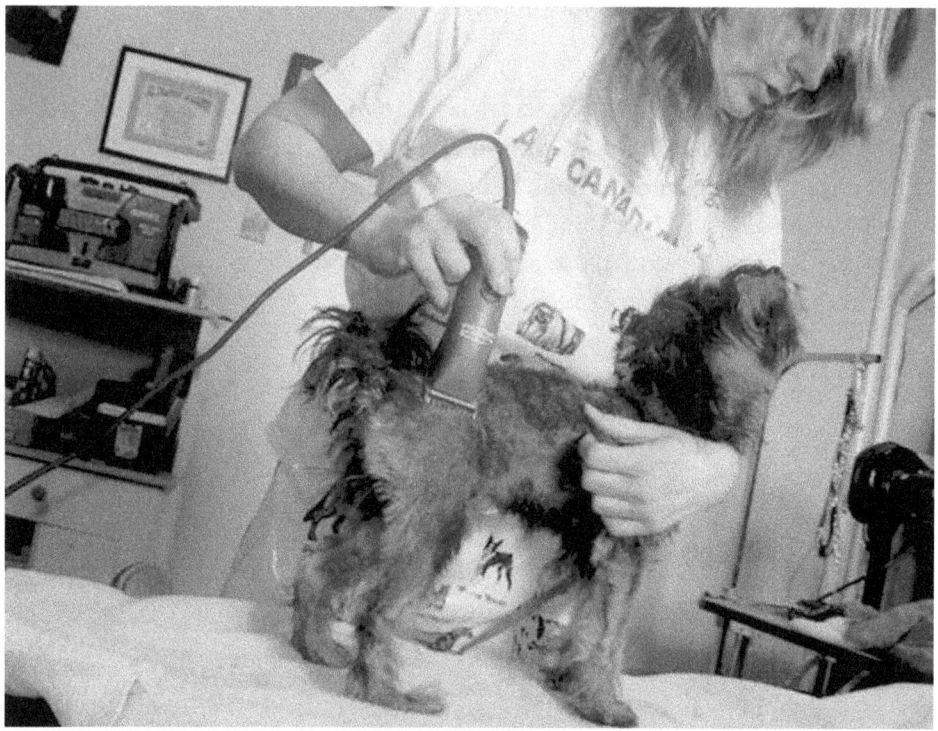

The puppy may struggle with his front legs, so give him time to calm down. He has already experienced you holding his legs, scissoring, and running the clippers over his legs without cutting any hair. He will settle quickly.

If the puppy panics when you put the clippers on the front legs, scissor the legs instead. This may be a puppy that will always need to have its legs scissored.

Clip between the pads on puppies that will need it done on a regular basis.

After the bath and dry, finish them according to the style you and the owner have decided on.

Face
This is the visit where you introduce the clippers to the corner of the eyes. Start below the corner and gradually work your way up to the corner of the eye. If the puppy is flailing and fighting, just scissor the corners of the eyes and between the eyes. It's better to be safe with scissors than risk cutting an eye with the clippers. Some dogs will never accept the clippers around the eyes, which is why it is very important to get them to accept the scissors. Puppies accept a narrow blade more readily than a full-sized blade, such as a 5/8 narrow blade. Every visit after, try with the clippers in the corners of the eyes. The more clipper work they have around their face and eyes, the sooner they will accept the clippers in the corners of their eyes.

What to expect
You will get some resistance to the clippers. The puppies will still offer resistance, but it won't be as severe as the second visit on most dogs. If the owners have been doing their homework, the puppy should be used to having his face, feet, and ears handled. The puppy may still be a bit finicky on the table, but will stop and stand when you tell him to and if he swings around to see what you are doing, he will settle quickly. The difference between the second and third visit always amazes me. It's like grooming a completely different dog.

The bath will go easier and will be less of a fight.

The final finish will have minimal spinning or swinging around.

The third visit is the end of the puppy program I run in my shop. When the puppy comes back for his fourth visit, he will usually stand on the table like a pro. Even the scared puppies will act this way. They have confidence, know what to expect and are confident that I won't hurt them. Most puppies are like this. Although I end the puppy program between 20 to 24 weeks, there are a few dogs that will be more difficult up until they are 8 months old, but they will still be very manageable after the puppy program. These dogs are either tough guy or wild personalities and are a bit slower on the maturity scale compared to other puppies of their age.

Troubleshooting
Body/legs
Some puppies will be fine with the clippers moving over their body backwards but will panic when you are actually cutting hair. I find that standing with these puppies pressed against you gives them the extra security they need to overcome the feel of the clippers cutting hair.

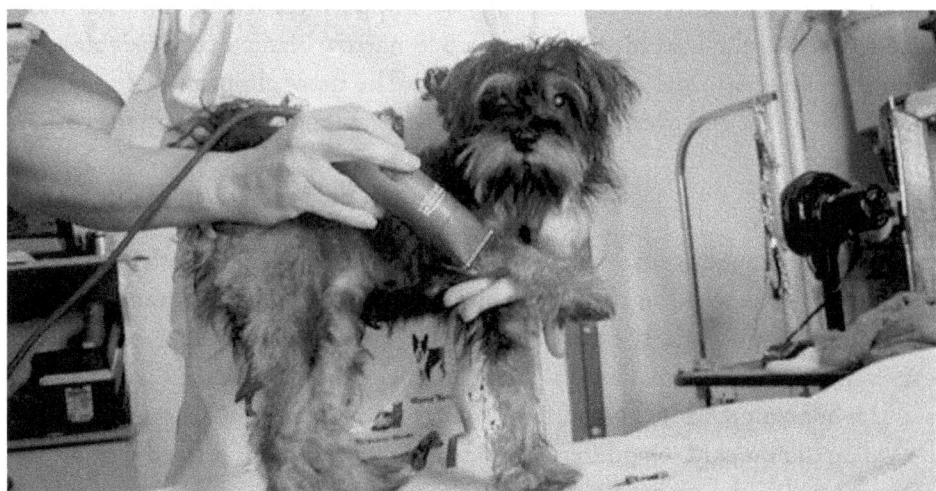

You may find that lifting them up on their rear legs, holding them on your forearm, and leaning against you will relax them and prevent them from swinging around or squirming.

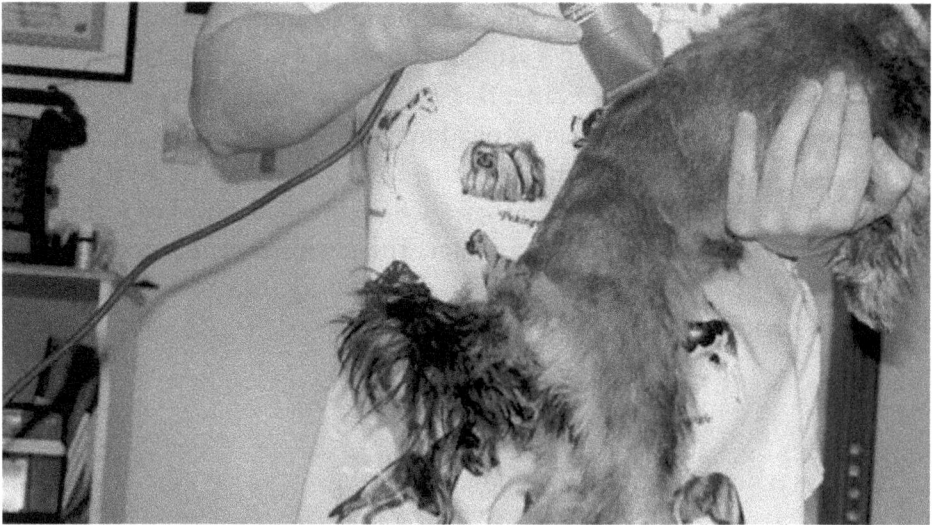

Feet
Follow the strategies for visit two.

Nails
The nails at this age are much thicker than at the first visit. Clipping the nails in the tub after the bath is easier on the puppy as the nails are softened by the water. I suggest *not* cutting the nails close to the quick. In my experience, the quick will often spider a tendril into the nail, and although you are not cutting into the quick, the nail still bleeds if you cut the tendril. I suggest cutting the nail or grinding the nail no closer than two or three millimetres from the quick.

Face
If the puppy fights the clippers around his eyes, use scissors. Every visit after, try the clippers around the eyes. Some puppies will take longer to accept having the clippers used around the eyes and on the face. Some puppies never accept it; this is why it is so important to teach the puppy to accept shears around the face and eyes so there is always a safe alternative to styling the face other than clippers.

Ears
If the puppy is jerky with ear plucking, finger pluck the ears. Never use an ear plucking tool on a puppy or dog that flails or jerks his head; you could inadvertently hurt the puppy. Some puppies and dogs have extremely sensitive ears. With these puppies, I start them on an alternative ear plucking routine where I pluck alternate ears each visit. This routine works very well for the ear sensitive dog. For puppies or dogs that attack when their ears are being plucked, I send them to the veterinarian.

Butt
Support the puppy on your forearm with the stomach resting on your arm. Manoeuvre your hand over the back so you can hold up the tail and clipper the around the anus area.

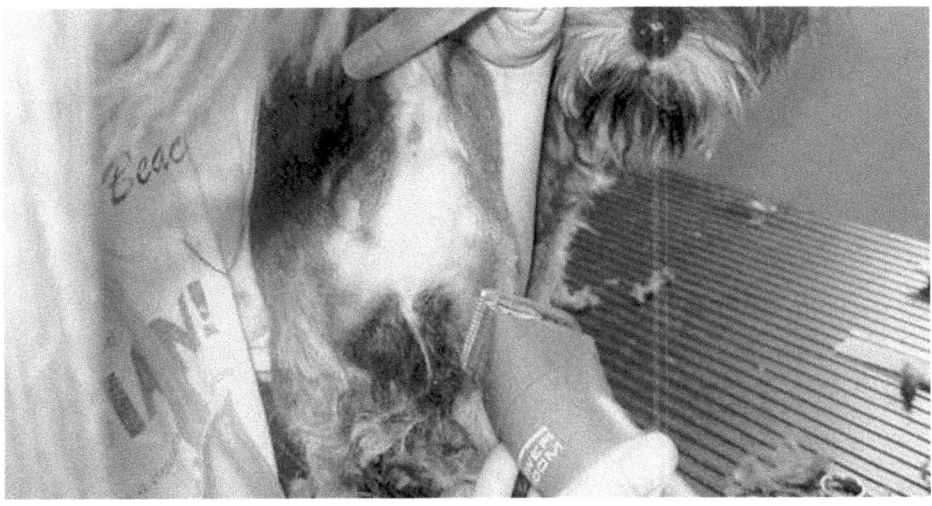

Chapter 8 Quick Glance Reference

First visit
    Meet and greet
    Table, *Stop*, and *Stand* exercises
    Touch and feel
    Grooming positions
    Equipment introduction
    Introduction to clippers on body, turned off
    Introduction to sound of clippers
    Clipping nails in lap
    Ear plucking
    Bath
    Cage and hand drying
    Scissor body, legs, and feet
    Scissor face
    Scissor ears

Second visit
    Meet and greet
    Touch and feeHydraulic table, ramp or steps, *Wait* and *Off* commands
    Table, *Stop*, *Stand*, and *Stay* exercises
    Positions
    Ear plucking
    Clip nails
    Introduction to sound of nail grinder
    Run clippers backwards over body, turned off
    Move clippers around body without touching the puppy
    Run clippers backwards over body, turned on
    Bath
    High velocity dryer/ cage dryer/hand drying
    Clipper fur flush with the pads
    Clipper poop chute/pee path
    Scissor body, legs, and feet
    Scissor face
    Scissor ears

Third visit
    Meet and greet
    Touch and feel
    Ear plucking
    Nail clipping
    Pre-bath clip
    Bath
    Drying
    Nail grinder on nails
    Style the puppy
    Face last
    Introduce the clippers on the face
    Finish ears

Chapter 9 Setting up The Program

You don't need any special equipment to set this program up. You now have the method for a three-part puppy program. Each visit should be done four weeks apart for maximum success. You can charge one fee at the beginning to cover all three visits or charge by the visit—the choice is yours. Typically, most groomers have a price for puppies. Your pricing will depend on your regular prices. I would suggest taking the price of a regular groom, splitting the price in half, and adding $5. This is your price for each of the three visits. In order to qualify for the pricing, the owners must understand that each visit must be four weeks apart (give or take a few days). This prevents some owners from dragging the program out to save money.

If they come in when the puppy is twelve weeks old, then they don't bring him back for seven weeks, I charge the price of a full groom. The puppy program has to be an agreement between you and the customer for it to be successful.

For puppies 16 weeks and older, I offer two puppy visits and combine week one and week two. I cut off the puppy program at 20 weeks. After 20 weeks, the puppy in is not eligible for the puppy program. They aren't typically puppies anymore after 20 weeks (five months). If you start a five month old puppy at week one of the puppy program, they will not finish the program until they are seven to eight months old. For puppies that aren't going to be groomed on a six to eight-week maintenance program (any short-haired or double-coated breeds), I only offer two puppy visits, rather than three. However, I do everything in the program except shaving them.

Chapter 10 Marketing the Program

Now you have the program running in your shop, but where are all the puppies? If the public doesn't know about your program, they can't access it. It's important to let people know about your special puppy program and all the benefits. I've included some effective ways to get the word out to your customers and potential customers.

Advertising
Advertise the puppy program in the local paper. Buy a business size ad or a medium block. Request that the advertisement be place on a page with other animal-related information. Placing an advertisement in the classifieds isn't very effective. If advertisements are expensive in your local paper, take out a smaller ad to announce the puppies that have passed the puppy program in your shop. This can be done once a month or every second month. You may get calls just out of curiosity as to what the program is.

When you purchase an ad in the yellow pages for your area, make sure the ad is worded as Puppy Program. Regular mail-outs to your clients, such as newsletters, is an inexpensive way to advertise any new programs. In your newsletter you can put congratulations to any puppy that has completed your program.

Take pictures. Display the pictures on a wall in your shop, or in the window, with the words Puppy Program Grads in large bold letters. (Have clients sign a release form for any photographs you take in your shop.)

Set up appointments with the veterinarians, dog trainers, and managers of the pet stores in your area that do not have a grooming shop on site. Explain to them the puppy program, why you started a puppy program, and how it benefits the puppy. Veterinarians and pet stores deal with puppies all the time, they are great word of mouth advertising for you. They will probably let you hang up a flyer for their customers or want some business cards to hand out.

Offer your program to the SPCA or any rescue societies for any puppies they have coming in. If you have a service dog training facility in your area, talk to them about the puppy program for their puppies that will be going to puppy homes before their final training.

Phone
When potential customers call to check prices, always ask the age of the dog. If it is a puppy, explain over the phone the puppy program and the cost of each visit. Emphasize the benefits for the puppy, owner and for future grooms.

Most people who price check will book with you, even if they phone other shops after the initial call. They are impressed and feel more confident bringing their new puppy to you because you are going to put their puppy through a special program. Other grooming shops offer a puppy bath and tidy, but very few offer a complete puppy program. How does this bring in income when you are charging much less than a regular groom? Ninety-five percent of owners with puppies that go through the puppy program will stay with you for regular grooming after. Word of mouth is the most effective form of advertising and they will tell family members, friends, and other people with puppies about the puppy program you run in your grooming shop.

Flyers and Brochures
Hang flyers in grocery stores, vet clinics, pet stores, and anywhere people with dogs go on a regular basis. Create a brochure for the puppy program to leave at the vets, pet stores, and dog trainers, and make sure you also have brochures about the puppy program in your shop for your regular clients to pass on to friends and family who have acquired a new puppy.

If your shop has a street window, hang a poster announcing the puppy program and remember to briefly describe it on the poster and for people to phone or come into the shop for more information.

Flyers advertising puppies for sale are a great way to spread the word about the puppy program. Take their number and ask if you can give them some brochures to give to any new owners that purchase their puppies. I usually offer a discounted full groom for their dog in exchange for handing out brochures.

Business Cards
List the puppy program on your business cards. If there is not enough room to list all your services on the front of your business card, utilize the back of the card.

Give something back

When the puppies are finished the puppy program, send the puppy home with a certificate of achievement or diploma for completing the program. Owners love that their puppy has passed (every puppy passes) and has a certificate to go home with. Puppy report cards are also a cute marketing tool for the program. You can give one each session, outlining what the puppy learned and how the puppy did during each exercise. You can also just give a final report card with notes for all three visits, to accompany the certificate. Although you may not think of this as marketing, it is a strong marketing tool. Many owners will frame their certificate or put it on their refrigerator where everyone who comes to visit can see it. If the report card is upbeat and humorous, they will laugh and show it to friends and family.

Take a picture, I find the best pictures are in the bath when the puppy is wet and full of soap. Print out a copy for the owners to go with the certificate and report card. Word will spread and remember, word of mouth is the most effective form of advertising.

Puppy packages for the first visit can be an excellent information resource for the owner. Packages can include a puppy treat, information about vaccinations, housebreaking, socialization, homework pages to send home with the puppy, and of course your business card or refrigerator magnet for your business.

Chapter 11 Toes and Tails

As I said earlier, grooming a puppy is like painting a picture during an earthquake. With some puppies, such as the wild ones, you'll feel like you're on a merry-go-round during that earthquake. Patience is definitely a key when grooming a puppy, but it takes skill as well. I have given you the tools to safely teach a puppy how to be groomed and to maintain your sanity.

I've added in this chapter some hints and tips that didn't fit anywhere in the book.

When not to groom a puppy
I explained the best time to start a puppy is at 12 weeks, but when do you say no to a puppy?

If you are female and experience PMS, do not groom a puppy at this time. Your patience level is very low and you will do more damage than good.

If you are hungry, eat before you tackle the puppy. Hunger will decrease your patience level.

Do not groom a puppy if you have any highly stressed dogs in the shop. The stress will transfer to the puppy.

If you have any anger issues, do not groom puppies. If you don't like puppies, don't groom them.

If the puppy hasn't had any vaccinations, refuse to groom it until the owners get the vaccinations. You want the puppy to be as safe as possible.

If the owners tell you the puppy has any signs of coughing, vomiting, or diarrhea, refuse the puppy until it is healthy. You want to keep you shop as safe as possible for other dogs.

Finishing
When the puppy is finished, put his collar on him, and then let him run around for a bit to fluff out. Bring the puppy back to the table to even out any stray hairs. When you are sure that you are completely finished, put on the bandana or bows.

The collar and bandanas or bows act as a signal to the puppy. When the collar is put on they realize they are almost finished. When the bandana or bows go on, they know they are done and you won't muck around with them anymore. If you don't decorate dogs in your shop, put on their collar when you are finished evening out any stray hairs. The collar becomes the signal that they are done.

Using food
Food is one of the best ways to distract a puppy. Food should be tiny pieces. If the puppy has a full stomach, food is useless. Use food as a distraction or as an unexpected treat. Praise should always be the constant.

Notes to home groomers
If you are a puppy owner planning to groom your dog at home, I have a few requests.

When you groom, please groom your whole dog, including clipping the nails and plucking the ears. It is very frustrating for groomers when a dog that has only been home-groomed comes in once a year with a year's growth on the nails or in the ears. If you are not comfortable with plucking the ears or clipping the nails, take the dog to the groomer or your veterinarian at least every six weeks to have it done.

When you bath your puppy at home, please make sure you rinse all the shampoo out. If you use a glass or jug to rinse, swish the fur with your fingers to thoroughly rinse the soap. I can't tell you how many dogs I get that are bathed regularly at home, but I have to rinse shampoo out before I even bath the dog. Shampoo left in can dry the coat and make the dog extremely itchy.

Brush your dog regularly. If you are unsure as to which brush to use for your breed of dog, ask your groomer. If you are unsure as to how to properly brush your dog, again, ask your groomer to show you.

Know your limitations. Grooming a puppy or dog isn't as easy as it looks.

The dog always wins
I often hear from owners and other groomers, "But then the dog wins." Understand that in a grooming shop, the dog always wins because the dog always gets to go home. The question is will the dog be happy to come back?

I see grooming as a partnership rather than me dominating the dog and forcing it to my will. The beginning of that partnership is taught in this book with puppies. The partnership starts in the first visit, is tested in the second visit, and secured in the third visit. The partnership can be a positive partnership that will create a win-win scenario for every groom after the puppy program or it can be a negative partnership in which the groomer will eventually refuse to see the dog.

The methods and strategies presented in this book are geared toward creating a positive partnership and creating a good dog to groom in the future.

About the Author

I have been fortunate to do what I wanted to do since I was a little girl—work with animals. My path has taken me down the road of veterinarian assistant for domestic and exotic pets, wildlife rehabilitation, animal rescue with different SPCAs, dog training, grooming, and now writing. There has always been one constant in this path we call life—I've always had at least one dog walking with me, following me, or causing me to chase them. My life as a dog trainer started in the early 1980s when I was asked to stay on as an apprentice after taking Quila, my Shepherd cross, through obedience classes. From there I started competing in obedience, conformation, agility, and fly ball with Toshi, Kitt, Jake, and Boo. After attaining an instructor's certification for dog obedience, I held a variety of pet obedience classes in different places I lived. My specialization became training dogs deemed untrainable. Landing jobs in veterinary clinics kept me busy for ten years and eventually led me into pet grooming in the 1990s. Combining my knowledge and skill as a dog trainer with my experience from veterinary clinics, I began to specialize in the dogs that were refused by other groomers.

I love grooming dogs and cats and still specialize in behaviour dogs both in training and in grooming.

My husband and three children are my heroes for bandaging my fingers when my reflexes aren't quite fast enough, holding up tails for me to shave under, and bribing with a variety of food and toys. Skye, my current Belgian Sheepdog, is my four-legged wonder who always makes me shake my head and laugh at his antics. Willow and Storm, who swack me whenever I'm slow on giving them tuna, keep me grounded with their cat demands.

My current grooming shop is The Garage Grooming Shop located in Sylvan Lake, Alberta. Stop by my web site at www.animaldancers.com and say hi.

Photo Credits

Photos were taken in shop by Jackie Larocque, Stephan Larocque, Tachara Larocque, Sulley Larocque and Kiara Larocque.

The Stars

Mogli
A cautious boxer cross. After much coaxing and playing, he realized the table was fun and we had trouble keeping him off it.

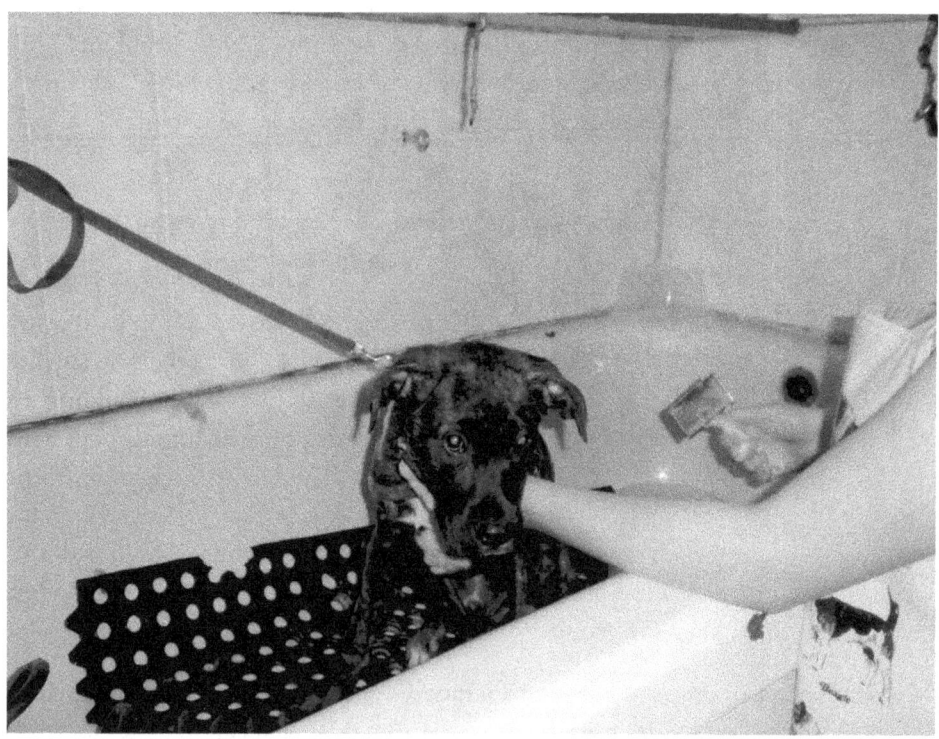

Jingles
Laid back surfer Shih Tzu who hated his face and ears being touched. He is on an alternate ear plucking program and falls asleep now when styling his face.

Truffles
Cautious love puppy. He needed extra time when new things were introduced. He now struts into the shop and is confident and happy to be groomed.

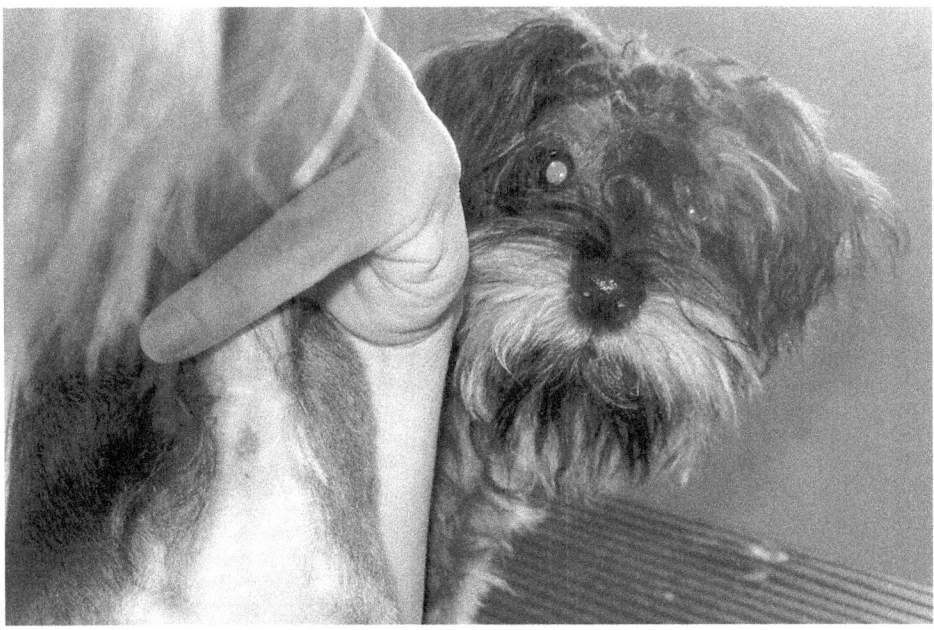

Cookie
Royalty Shih Tzu, born without a tail, she acts like a princess and expects all to bow to her.

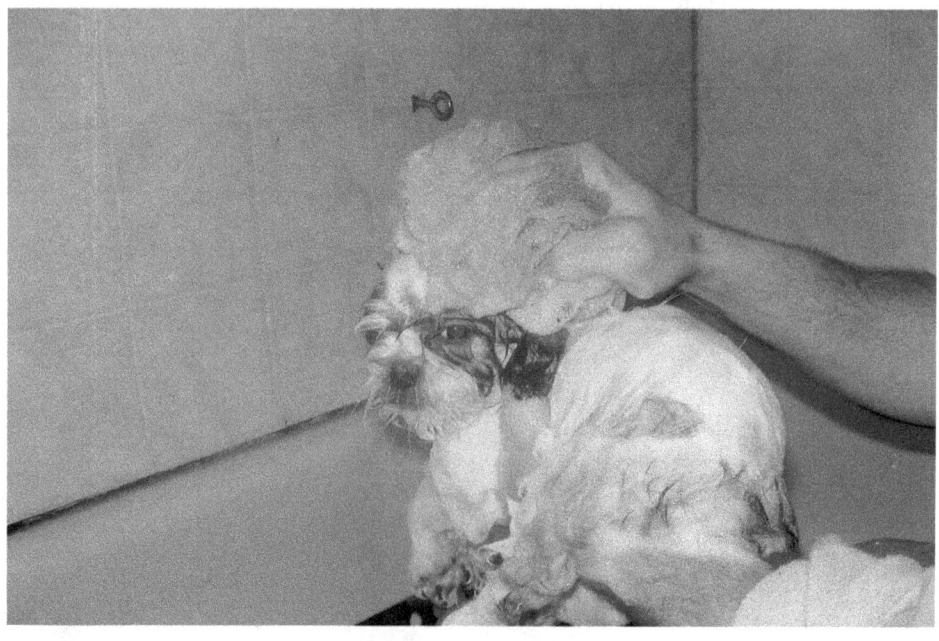

Miley
Tough girl Shih Tzu. She was attacking when anyone went near her face at 12 weeks old. She is now one of the best dogs around her face.

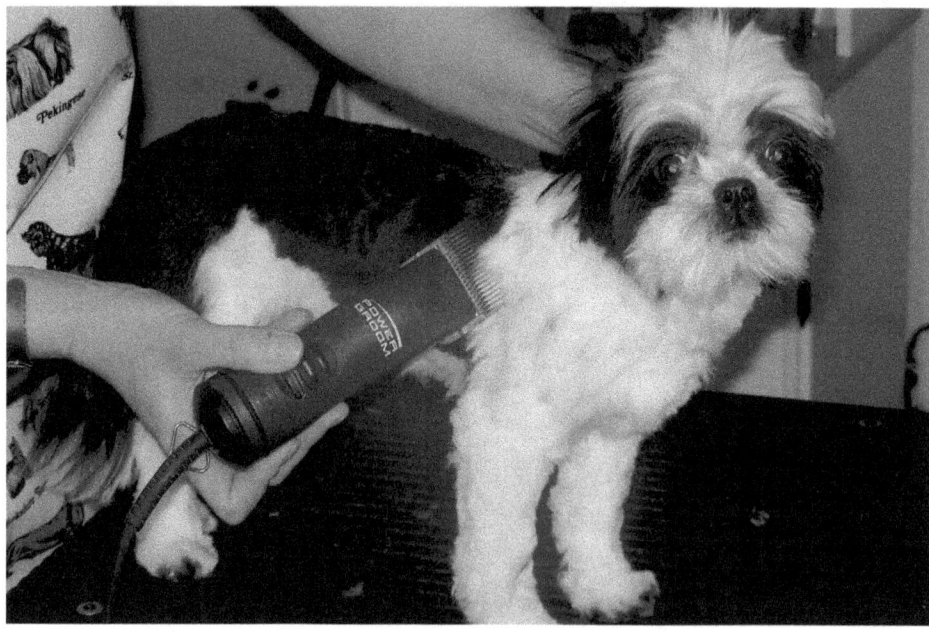

Baxter
Scared Yorkie puppy. By the third puppy visit, Baxter was much more relaxed, wasn't overdramatic and had fun.

Tucker
Maltese cross love puppy, with a bit of cautious mixed in. A sweet puppy that squeaked like a squeaky toy.

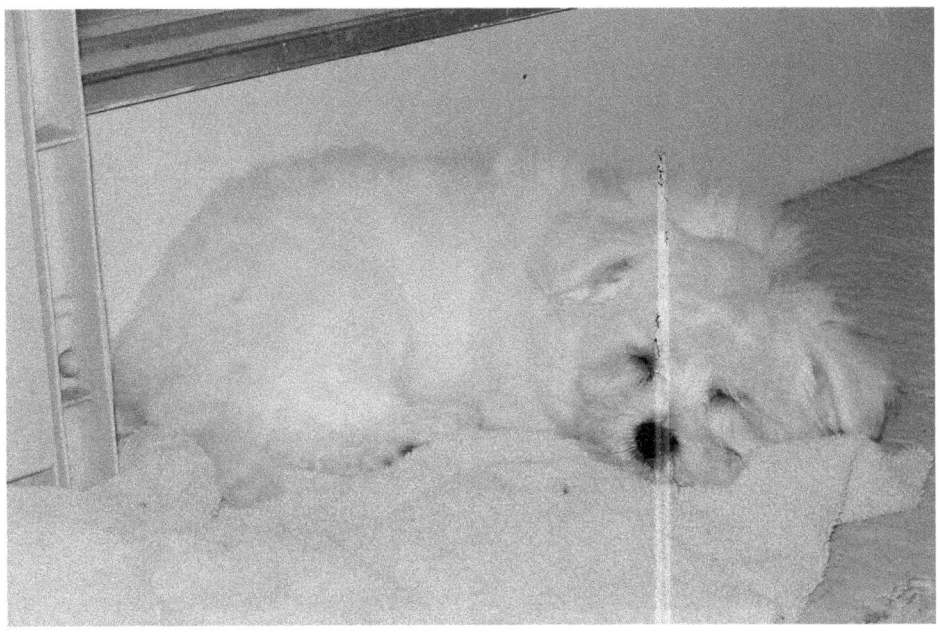

Maya
A wild Labrador. She tried to eat everything in the shop. Still tries to eat the water out of the hose.

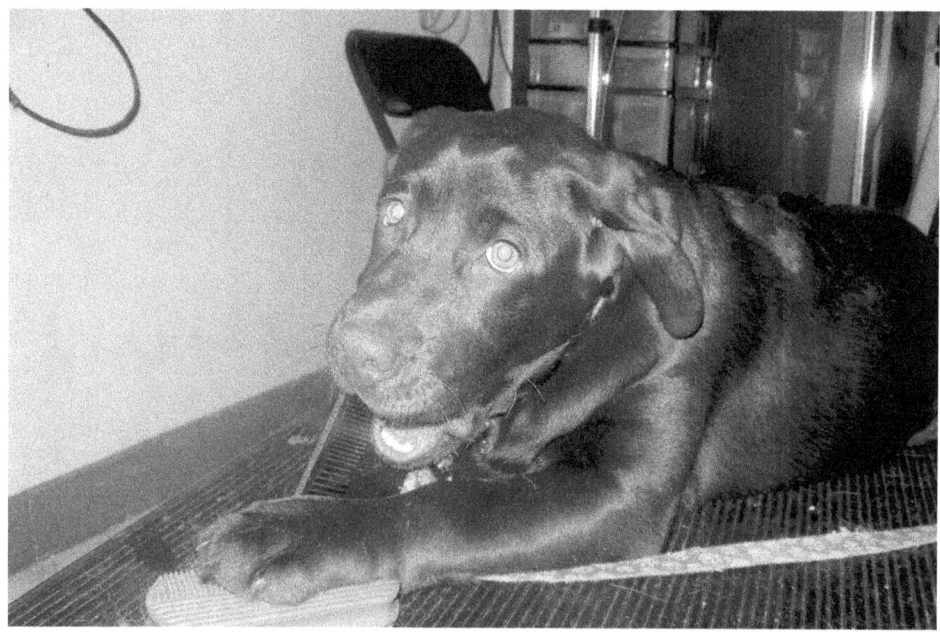

Jasper
A wild love cocker spaniel. By the third visit, he kept his wildness to the floor.

Max
A love Yorkie who grins, kisses and waves his paws. He graciously modeled for the sausage puppy even though he doesn't need to be sausage rolled for his face.

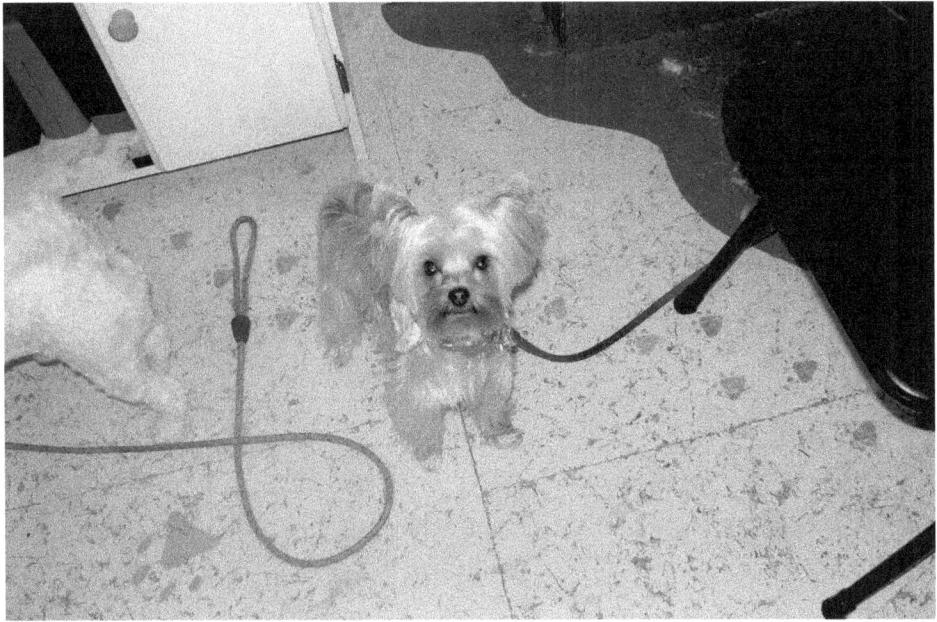

Resources

Recommended Reading

The Art Of Raising A Puppy
The Monks of New Skeet, 1991
An in depth book about choosing a puppy and raising it.

Don't Shoot The Dog, The New Art of Teaching and Training
Karen Pryor, 1999
Training your dog, husband, or roommate using positive motivational technique.

Click for Grooming, Handling and treatment
Karen McCarthy, 2006.
A level 2 clicker training course to shape behaviour for grooming.

How to Speak Dog
Stanley Coren, 2000,
The study of how dogs communicate and how we can learn and use their language.

Why Does My Dog Act That Way?
Stanley Coren, 2006,
A guide to the reasons a dog acts a certain way, explaining how external influences create your dogs personality.

The Healing Touch for Dogs, the Proven massage Program
Dr Michael W. Fox, 2004 An excellent book on where and how to touch and massage a dog.

Don't Dump The Dog
Randy Grim with Melinda Roth, 2009
Simple solutions to common behaviour problems. Very humorous stories about rescued dogs and reasons owners 'dump' dogs.

Web Sites

JKL Training Academy
www.jklgrooming.com
An internationally recognized long distance grooming course that takes you step by step to learn dog and cat grooming for all breeds.

Volhard Dog Training and Nutrition
www.volhard.com
A dog training and nutrition website with detailed explanation on temperaments and testing.

Tellington Touch
www.ttouch.com
An excellent site for those who are investigating animal massage.

Stacy's Wag 'n' Train
www.wagntrain.com
A dog training site that explains in detail conditional training.

The Michael Ellis School For Dog Trainers
www.michaelellisschool.com
A school for trainers and dog owners who want to explore operant training techniques in different facets of training.

Animal dancers
www.animaldancers.com
The authors website

National Dog Groomers Association
www.nationaldoggroomers.com
A website for dog groomers with information on certification, seminars and workshops.

IPG, International Professional Groomers, Inc.
ipgcmg.org
An organization to promote the continued education of pet groomers.

Downloadable puppy packs for your puppy program are available.

With a single download, you can print off the following:

- Homework pages for your clients
- Housebreaking tips
- Report cards
- Brochures for your puppy program

Each is available individually or as a whole pack. You print copies as you need them and the amount you need for as long as you want.

www.animaldancers.com/wetwildpuppygrooming.html

Come say hi at Jackie's website at www.animaldancers.com and be sure to check out other publications available to aid you in marketing your business.

ALSO BY JACKIE LAROCQUE

Hot Oil Treatments For Dogs

Learn the benefits of hot oil treatments for dogs in this comprehensive manual. Step by step instructions in applying hot oil in a safe manner. Recipes you can easily mix in your shop or at home and why hot oil treatments are beneficial for all dogs.

COMING IN THE FALL OF 2011

Dog Parties

From puppy parties to birthday parties, from dog owners to dog professionals, join in the fun of planning or hosting a party. Dog parties is packed full of games, recipes and strategies to have parties for all to enjoy.

www.ingramcontent.com/pod-product-compliance
Lightning Source LLC
Chambersburg PA
CBHW080345170426
43194CB00014B/2696